中国国学经典学习丛书
Books on Classics of Chinese Studies

漫画《论语》全译本 下

The Analects of Confucius with Illustrations
A complete translated version 2

主编：于 健　　执行主编：赵 昱

Printed in China

Donated by Hanban, China

北京语言大学出版社
BEIJING LANGUAGE AND CULTURE
UNIVERSITY PRESS

总 顾 问：宁继鸣

总 策 划：王志民

主　　编：于　健

执行主编：赵　昱

英文翻译：于　健　侯萍萍

顾　　问：傅永军　黄历鸿　颜炳罡　王均林　陈　川　费文鸿
　　　　　张清旻　马晓乐　张艾瑛　丁建奎　M·其米德策耶

美　　术：张其波　王玉娟　李　孔　董宜君　陈　思　陈根生

前 言

孔子（公元前551—前479年）是中国历史上伟大的思想家、教育家，也是世界历史上一位伟大的学者。他创建的儒家学说，成为中国传统文化的主体。他为中华文明乃至世界文明做出了不朽的贡献，联合国教科文组织把他列为世界十大历史名人之一。

两千多年来，《论语》一直是中国人必读的经典。这部书是孔子的弟子和后学弟子关于孔子及其弟子言行的记录，全书共20篇，集中体现了孔子的政治主张、伦理观念及教育原则，其核心思想是"仁"。

《论语》表达方式言简意赅，很多都是孔子触景生情、有感而发的议论，读起来很亲切，适合利用漫画形式阅读。

《漫画〈论语〉》（全译本）中英文版将《论语》原文、现代汉语译文、英语译文及漫画融为一体，并将原文加注汉语拼音，原文全部配有朗读录音，方便读者理解、背诵。

同各国古代经典一样，对《论语》的解读至今未止，所以，读者对书中一些内容的不解是很正常的。鉴于《论语》中大部分内容是中国人家喻户晓的，学习《论语》并熟读之，是汉语学习者很重要的一项任务。《漫画〈论语〉》（全译本）是学习汉语和中国文化的理想读物。

Foreword

Confucius (551 – 479 BC) is considered a great thinker and educator in Chinese history and one of the great scholars in the world history. He was the founder of Confucianism, which constitutes a major part of traditional Chinese culture. He has made tremendous contributions to the civilization of China and even the world, therefore, he was listed by UNESCO as one of the world's top ten historical figures.

The Analects of Confucius, hereafter referred to as *The Analects*, has always been a classic for Chinese people over the past two thousand years. It is a collection of Confucius and his followers' words and records of their deeds, compiled by his disciples. *The Analects*, consisting of 20 chapters, embodies Confucius' political ideas, ethics, and principles of education. The core value of *The Analects* is "benevolence".

The Analects features a concise and comprehensive style, with many of the passages recording Confucius' remarks sparked by various scenes or occasions. It reads easily and close-to-life and is certainly suitable for illustrations.

The Analects of Confucius with Illustrations (A complete translated version) integrates the original ancient Chinese version with a modern Chinese version and a modern English version, and is enhanced with illustrations. To facilitate readers' understanding and reciting, the book also provides Chinese *pinyin* and the recording for the original ancient Chinese version.

Like the ancient classics of all nations, *The Analects* has been generating constant interpretations. Consequently, readers are required to constantly learn and update their understanding of this classic. Since most passages from *The Analects* are widely known among Chinese people, it is important for non-Chinese interested in the Chinese language and culture to familiarize themselves with *The Analects*. *The Analects of Confucius with Illustrations* (A complete translated version) is ideal in helping people to learn the Chinese language and culture.

目 录

先进第十一 …………………… 1

颜渊第十二 …………………… 33

子路第十三 …………………… 60

宪问第十四 …………………… 95

卫灵公第十五 ………………… 142

季氏第十六 …………………… 185

阳货第十七 …………………… 204

微子第十八 …………………… 233

子张第十九 …………………… 247

尧曰第二十 …………………… 274

Contents

Chapter Eleven 1

Chapter Twelve 33

Chapter Thirteen 60

Chapter Fourteen 95

Chapter Fifteen 142

Chapter Sixteen 185

Chapter Seventeen 204

Chapter Eighteen 233

Chapter Nineteen 247

Chapter Twenty 274

xiān jìn dì shí yī
先进第十一
CHAPTER ELEVEN

先进第十一　Chapter Eleven

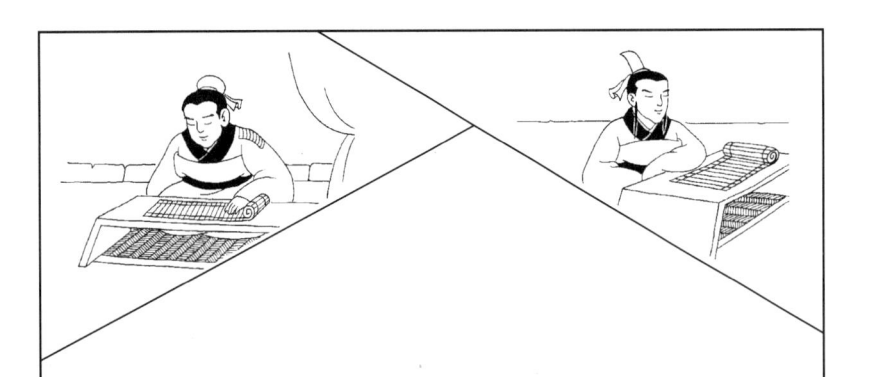

【释义】

孔子说:"先学习礼乐而后做官的,是原来没有爵禄的平民;先当了官再学习礼乐的,是原来就有爵禄的君子。如果要选用人才,那我主张用先学习礼乐的人。"

【英译】

The Master said, "Those who had learned rituals and music before they became officials are of humble origins, while those who had learned rituals and music after they became officials are from aristocratic families. In selecting talents, I'd prefer the former."

孔子说:"如果要选用人才,那我主张用先学习礼乐的人。"

The Master said, "In selecting talents, I'd prefer those who had learned rituals and music (before they became officials)."

11.1
zǐ yuē　　　xiān jìn yú lǐ yuè　　yě rén yě　　hòu jìn yú lǐ yuè
子曰:"先进于礼乐,野人也;后进于礼乐,
jūn zǐ yě　　rú yòng zhī　　zé wú cóng xiān jìn
君子也。如用之,则吾从先进。"

Chapter Eleven 先进第十一

孔子说："跟随我在陈、蔡两国受困的学生，都不在我的门下了。"

The Master said, "Among my disciples who followed me from the State of Chen to the State of Cai, none is with me any more."

【释义】

孔子说："跟随我在陈、蔡两国受困的学生，都不在我的门下了。"

【英译】

The Master said, "Among my disciples who followed me from the State of Chen to the State of Cai, none is with me any more."

11.2 zǐ yuē cóng wǒ yú chén cài zhě jiē bù jí mén yě
子曰："从我于陈、蔡者，皆不及门也。

3

先进第十一　Chapter Eleven

孔子说："我的学生中，道德修养好的有：颜渊，闵子骞，冉伯牛，仲弓。"

The Master said, "Among my disciples, virtuous in conduct were Yan Yuan, Min Ziqian, Ran Boniu and Zhong Gong."

11.3

dé xíng　yán yuān　mǐn zǐ qiān　rǎn bó niú　zhòng gōng　yán yǔ
德行：颜渊，闵子骞，冉伯牛，仲弓；言语：
zǎi wǒ　zǐ gòng　zhèng shì　rǎn yǒu　jì lù　wén xué　zǐ
宰我，子贡；政事：冉有，季路；文学：子
yóu　zǐ xià
游，子夏。

【释义】

孔子的学生中，道德修养好的有：颜渊，闵子骞，冉伯牛，仲弓；善于辞令的有：宰我，子贡；善于政事的有：冉有，季路；文化修养好的有：子游，子夏。

【英译】

Among Confucius' disciples, virtuous in conduct were Yan Yuan, Min Ziqian, Ran Boniu and Zhong Gong; eloquent in speech were Zai Wo and Zi Gong; competent in governance were Ran You and Ji Lu; and accomplished in literature were Zi You and Zi Xia.

Chapter Eleven　先进第十一

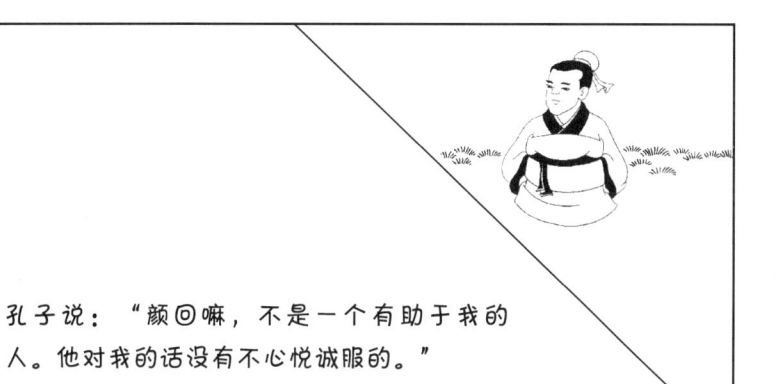

孔子说："颜回嘛，不是一个有助于我的人。他对我的话没有不心悦诚服的。"

The Master said, "Yan Hui is not of help to me. He is pleased with and convinced by everything I say."

【释义】

孔子说："颜回嘛，不是一个有助于我的人。他对我的话没有不心悦诚服的。"

【英译】

The Master said, "Yan Hui is not of help to me. He is pleased with and convinced by everything I say."

11.4
zǐ yuē　　huí yě　　fēi zhù wǒ zhě yě　　yú wú yán wú suǒ bú yuè
子曰："回也，非助我者也。于吾言无所不说。"

先进第十一　Chapter Eleven

【释义】

孔子说:"闵子骞真孝啊!别人从不非议他父母兄弟称许他孝顺的话。"

【英译】

The Master said, "What a filial son Min Ziqian is! Everyone agrees with his father and brother's compliments about him."

孔子说:"闵子骞真孝啊!别人从不非议他父母兄弟称许他孝顺的话。"

The Master said, "What a filial son Min Ziqian is! Everyone agrees with his father and brother's compliments about him."

11.5

zǐ yuē　　　xiào zāi mǐn zǐ qiān　　rén bú jiàn yú qí fù mǔ kūn dì
子曰:"孝哉闵子骞!人不间于其父母昆弟

zhī yán
之言。"

Chapter Eleven 先进第十一

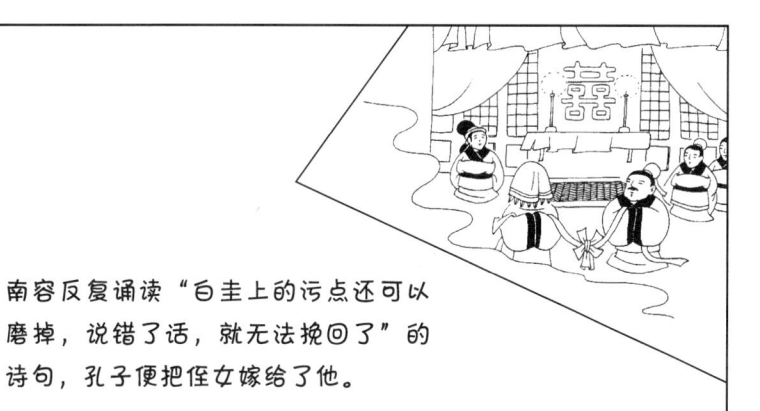

南容反复诵读"白圭上的污点还可以磨掉，说错了话，就无法挽回了"的诗句，孔子便把侄女嫁给了他。

Nan Rong repeatedly chanted the lines from *The Book of Songs* "One can wipe a stain off a white jade tablet, but cannot take back wrong remarks that have been made." The Master married his own niece to him.

【释义】

南容反复诵读"白圭上的污点还可以磨掉，说错了话，就无法挽回了"的诗句，孔子便把侄女嫁给了他。

【英译】

Nan Rong repeatedly chanted the lines from *The Book of Songs* "One can wipe a stain off a white jade tablet, but cannot take back wrong remarks that have been made." The Master married his own niece to him.

11.6 nán róng sān fù bái guī, kǒng zǐ yǐ qí xiōng zhī zǐ qì zhī

南容三复白圭，孔子以其兄之子妻之。

先进第十一　Chapter Eleven

孔子说："有个叫颜回的好学，可惜不幸短命死了。现在再没有这样好学的人了。"

The Master said, "There was Yan Hui who was very studious. Unfortunately he died at a young age. Now there is no one who loves learning as much as Yan Hui."

11.7

jì kāng zǐ wèn　　dì zǐ shú wéi hào xué　　kǒng zǐ duì yuē
季康子问："弟子孰为好学？"孔子对曰：
yǒu yán huí zhě hào xué　bú xìng duǎn mìng sǐ yǐ　jīn yě zé wú
"有颜回者好学，不幸短命死矣。今也则亡。"

【释义】

季康子问道："弟子中谁最好学？"孔子回答说："有个叫颜回的好学，可惜不幸短命死了。现在再没有这样好学的人了。"

【英译】

Ji Kangzi asked, "Who is the most studious among your disciples?" The Master answered, "There was Yan Hui. Unfortunately he died at a young age. Now there is no one who loves learning as much as Yan Hui."

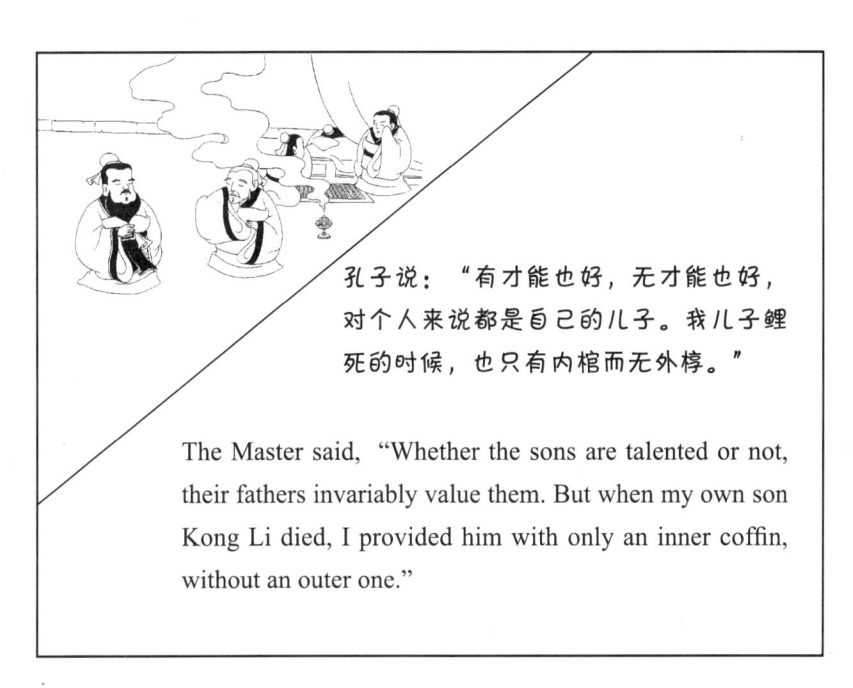

Chapter Eleven 先进第十一

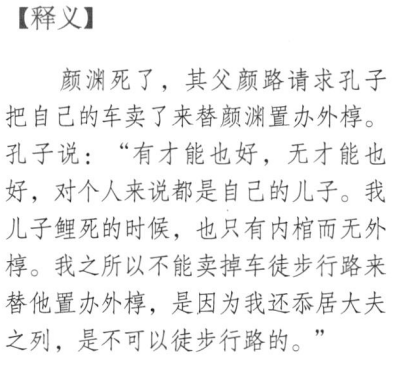

孔子说："有才能也好，无才能也好，对个人来说都是自己的儿子。我儿子鲤死的时候，也只有内棺而无外椁。"

The Master said, "Whether the sons are talented or not, their fathers invariably value them. But when my own son Kong Li died, I provided him with only an inner coffin, without an outer one."

11.8

yán yuān sǐ　　yán lù qǐng zǐ zhī chē yǐ wéi zhī guǒ　　zǐ yuē　　cái
颜渊死，颜路请子之车以为之椁。子曰："才
bù cái　　yì gè yán qí zǐ yě　　lǐ yě sǐ　　yǒu guān ér wú guǒ
不才，亦各言其子也。鲤也死，有棺而无椁。
wú bù tú xíng yǐ wéi zhī guǒ　　yǐ wú cóng dà fū zhī hòu　　bù kě tú
吾不徒行以为之椁，以吾从大夫之后，不可徒
xíng yě
行也。"

【释义】

颜渊死了，其父颜路请求孔子把自己的车卖了来替颜渊置办外椁。孔子说："有才能也好，无才能也好，对个人来说都是自己的儿子。我儿子鲤死的时候，也只有内棺而无外椁。我之所以不能卖掉车徒步行路来替他置办外椁，是因为我还忝居大夫之列，是不可以徒步行路的。"

【英译】

When Yan Yuan died, his father Yan Lu asked the Master to sell his carriage and use the money to buy an outer coffin for his son. The Master answered, "Whether the sons are talented or not, their fathers invariably value them. But when my own son Kong Li died, I provided him with only an inner coffin, without an outer one. I didn't sell my carriage to buy him an outer coffin because as a former official, it would have been improper for me to go around on foot."

Note: Burying one's parents or children beyond one's ability was in defiance of etiquette.

先进第十一　Chapter Eleven

【释义】

颜渊死了。孔子说:"咳!老天爷要我的命了!老天爷要我的命了!"

【英译】

When Yan Yuan passed away, the Master cried, "Heaven is claiming my life! Heaven is claiming my life!"

颜渊死了。孔子说:"咳!老天爷要我的命了!"

When Yan Yuan passed away, the Master cried, "Heaven is claiming my life!"

11.9 yán yuān sǐ　　zǐ yuē　　　yī　tiān sàng yú　tiān sàng yú
颜 渊 死。子 曰:"噫! 天 丧 予! 天 丧 予!"

Chapter Eleven　先进第十一

颜渊死了。孔子说："我是悲伤过度了吗？不为这样的人悲痛欲绝还为谁呢？"

Yan Yuan passed away. The Master said, "Am I excessively grieved? If I am not grieved for him, who will I be grieved for?"

11.10
yán yuān sǐ　zǐ kū zhī tòng　cóng zhě yuē　zǐ tòng yǐ　yuē
颜渊死，子哭之恸。从者曰："子恸矣。"曰：
yǒu tòng hū　fēi fú rén zhī wèi tòng ér shuí wèi
"有恸乎？非夫人之为恸而谁为？"

【释义】

颜渊死了，孔子为他哭丧，悲痛欲绝。跟随的人说："先生悲伤得有些过分了。"孔子说："我是悲伤过度了吗？不为这样的人悲痛欲绝还为谁呢？"

【英译】

When Yan Yuan passed away, the Master wept in deep sorrow. His followers said, "Master, you are excessively grieved." The Master replied, "Am I? If I am not grieved for him, who will I be grieved for?"

先进第十一　Chapter Eleven

颜渊死了，孔子不赞同用丰厚的礼来葬颜渊。

When Yan Yuan died, Confucius didn't agree to give him a lavish burial.

11.11
yán yuān sǐ　　mén rén yù hòu zàng zhī　　zǐ yuē　　　bù kě
颜渊死，门人欲厚葬之。子曰："不可。"
mén rén hòu zàng zhī　　zǐ yuē　　huí yě　　shì yú yóu fù yě　　yú
门人厚葬之。子曰："回也，视予犹父也，予
bù dé shì yóu zǐ yě　　fēi wǒ yě　　fú èr sān zǐ yě
不得视犹子也。非我也，夫二三子也。"

【释义】

颜渊死了，孔子的学生们想用丰厚的礼来葬颜渊。孔子说："不可以。"

学生们还是用丰厚的礼葬了颜渊。孔子说："颜回看待我如同父亲，我却不能看待他如同儿子。不是我要这样的呀，是那些学生要这样的呀。"

【英译】

When Yan Yuan died, his fellow disciples wanted to give him a lavish burial. The Master said, "You should not do that."

But the disciples did it anyway. The Master remarked, "Yan Hui, you had treated me as your father, but I wasn't able to treat you like my own son. It's not my fault, but that of your fellow disciples."

Chapter Eleven 先进第十一

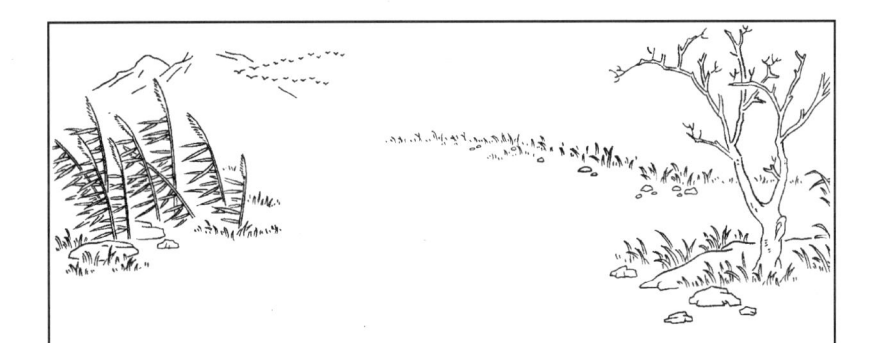

孔子说："还不知道生，又怎么知道死呢？"

The Master said, "You don't yet understand life, how can you understand death?"

11.12
jì lù wèn shì guǐ shén　　zǐ yuē　　wèi néng shì rén　　yān néng shì guǐ
季路问事鬼神。子曰："未能事人，焉能事鬼？"
yuē　　gǎn wèn sǐ　　yuē　　wèi zhī shēng　　yān zhī sǐ
曰："敢问死？"曰："未知生，焉知死？"

【释义】

子路问服事鬼神的事。孔子说："还不能服事活人，又怎能服事鬼神呢？"

子路又说："敢问死是怎么回事？"孔子说："还不知道生，又怎么知道死呢？"

【英译】

Ji Lu (Zi Lu) asked about ways to serve the ghosts and spirits. The Master said, "You don't yet know how to serve human beings, how can you possibly serve ghosts and spirits?"

Zi Lu then asked, "May I venture to ask about death?" The Master answered, "You don't yet understand life, how can you understand death?"

先进第十一　Chapter Eleven

【释义】

　　闵子骞侍奉在孔子身旁，显出恭敬正直的样子；子路则显出刚强的样子；冉有、子贡则显出和乐的样子。孔子很高兴，但又说："像仲由那样，恐怕会得不到善终。"

【英译】

　　When attending the Master, Min Ziqian looked respectful and upright, Zi Lu resolute, Ran You and Zi Gong genial. The Master was very pleased. But then he said, "I'm afraid a man like Zhong You (Zi Lu) may not die a natural death."

孔子说："像仲由那样，恐怕会得不到善终。"

The Master said, "I'm afraid a man like Zhong You may not die a natural death."

11.13
_{mǐn zǐ shì cè} _{yín yín rú yě} _{zǐ lù} _{hàng hàng rú yě} _{rǎn}
闵子侍侧，訚訚如也；子路，行行如也；冉
_{yǒu} _{zǐ gòng} _{kǎn kǎn rú yě} _{zǐ lè} _{ruò yóu yě} _{bù}
有、子贡，侃侃如也。子乐。"若由也，不
_{dé qí sǐ rán}
得其死然。"

Chapter Eleven 先进第十一

孔子说："闵子骞这个人不讲话则已，一讲话正中要害。"

The Master said, "Min Ziqian is a man who seldom speaks, but once he does, he speaks right to the point."

11.14
lǔ rén wéi cháng fǔ　　mǐn zǐ qiān yuē　　réng jiù guàn　　rú zhī hé
鲁人为长府。闵子骞曰："仍旧贯，如之何？
hé bì gǎi zuò　　zǐ yuē　　fú rén bù yán　　yán bì yǒu zhòng
何必改作？"子曰："夫人不言，言必有中。"

【释义】

鲁国人翻修长府。闵子骞说："照老样子，怎么样？为什么一定要改建呢？"孔子说："这个人不讲话则已，一讲话正中要害。"

【英译】

The people of the State of Lu were planning to remodel their treasury. Min Ziqian said, "Why not just restore it? Why must it be remodeled?" The Master remarked, "Here is a man who seldom speaks, but once he does, he speaks right to the point."

先进第十一　Chapter Eleven

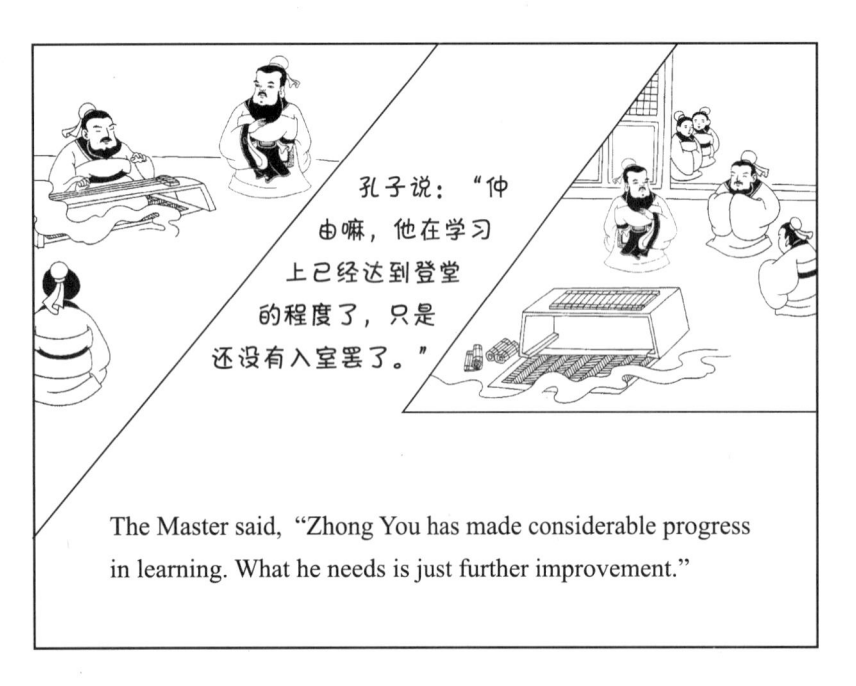

【释义】

孔子说："仲由弹瑟，为什么在我这里弹呢？"孔子的学生们因此都不尊敬子路。孔子便说："仲由嘛，他在学习上已经达到登堂的程度了，只是还没有入室罢了。"

【英译】

The Master said, "In terms of playing the *se*, Zhong You (Zi Lu) is not skillful enough to perform in my place." The other disciples began to show disrespect to Zi Lu. The Master then said, "Zhong You has made considerable progress in learning. What he needs is just further improvement."

Note: *Se* is a kind of Chinese musical instrument.

11.15
zǐ yuē　　yóu zhī sè　　xī wèi yú qiū zhī mén　　mén rén bú jìng
子曰："由之瑟，奚为于丘之门？"门人不敬
zǐ lù　　zǐ yuē　　yóu yě shēng táng yǐ　　wèi rù yú shì yě
子路。子曰："由也升堂矣，未入于室也。"

Chapter Eleven 先进第十一

孔子说:"过头和不足是一样的。"

The Master said, "Going too far is just as bad as not going far enough."

11.16
zǐ gòng wèn　　shī yǔ shāng yě shú xián　　zǐ yuē　　shī yě guò
子贡问:"师与商也孰贤?"子曰:"师也过,
shāng yě bù jí
商也不及。"
yuē　　rán zé shī yù yú　　zǐ yuē　　guò yóu bù jí
曰:"然则师愈与?"子曰:"过犹不及。"

【释义】

子贡问道:"颛孙师和卜商谁强一些?"孔子说:"颛孙师过头,卜商不足。"

子贡说:"那么颛孙师强一些吗?"孔子说:"过头和不足是一样的。"

【英译】

Zi Gong asked, "Who is better, Zhuansun Shi or Bu Shang?" The Master answered, "Zhuansun Shi goes too far while Bu Shang does not go far enough."

Zi Gong then asked, "Does this mean Zhuansun Shi is better?" The Master said, "Going too far is just as bad as not going far enough."

17

先进第十一　Chapter Eleven

【释义】

季氏比周公还富有，而冉求还为他搜刮民财进而增加他的财富。孔子说："他不是我的弟子了。后生们尽管敲起鼓来声讨他好了。"

【英译】

The Ji family possessed greater wealth than even the Duke of Zhou, yet Ran Qiu was helping the Ji family to increase their wealth by raising taxes on the populace. The Master said, "Ran Qiu is no student of mine! You can attack him to the beating of the drums."

季氏比周公还富有，而冉求还为他搜刮民财进而增加他的财富。

The Ji family possessed greater wealth than even the Duke of Zhou, yet Ran Qiu was helping the Ji family to increase their wealth by raising taxes on the populace.

11.17
jì shì fù yú zhōu gōng　ér qiú yě wèi zhī jù liǎn ér fù yì zhī　zǐ
季氏富于周公，而求也为之聚敛而附益之。子
yuē　fēi wú tú yě　xiǎo zǐ míng gǔ ér gōng zhī　kě yě
曰："非吾徒也。小子鸣鼓而攻之，可也。"

Chapter Eleven 先进第十一

高柴愚直，曾参迟钝，颛孙师偏激，仲由鲁莽。

Gao Chai is dull, Zeng Shen slow, Zhuansun Shi radical, and Zhong You reckless.

【释义】

高柴愚直，曾参迟钝，颛孙师偏激，仲由鲁莽。

【英译】

Gao Chai is dull, Zeng Shen slow, Zhuansun Shi radical, and Zhong You reckless.

11.18
chái yě yú， shēn yě lǔ， shī yě pì， yóu yě yàn
柴也愚，参也鲁，师也辟，由也喭。

先进第十一　Chapter Eleven

【释义】

孔子说："颜回的学问道德差不多了，只是常常空乏困顿。端木赐不安身立命偏偏去经商，而货财不断增加，揣度行情常常猜中。"

【英译】

The Master said, "Yan Hui is considerably accomplished in both his scholarship and morality, yet he often suffers poverty and hardship. Duanmu Ci refuses to accept his lot and chooses to do business, and his profit accumulates as he often makes right speculations about the market."

孔子说："颜回的学问道德差不多了，只是常常空乏困顿。"

The Master said, "Yan Hui is considerably accomplished in both his scholarship and morality, yet he often suffers poverty and hardship."

11.19 子曰："回也其庶乎，屡空。赐不受命，而货殖焉，亿则屡中。"
（zǐ yuē： huí yě qí shù hū， lǚ kōng。 cì bú shòu mìng， ér huò zhí yān， yì zé lǚ zhòng。）

Chapter Eleven 先进第十一

子张问作为善人的准则。孔子说:"如果不踩着前人的足迹走,那么学问道德还没有完全修养到家。"

Zi Zhang asked about the norms for a good man. The Master said, "Without learning from others, one can never attain perfection in either scholarship or character."

【释义】

子张问作为善人的准则。孔子说:"如果不踩着前人的足迹走,那么学问道德还没有完全修养到家。"

【英译】

Zi Zhang asked about the norms for a good man. The Master said, "Without learning from others, one can never attain perfection in either scholarship or character."

11.20
zǐ zhāng wèn shàn rén zhī dào　　zǐ yuē　　bú jiàn jì　　yì bú rù yú
子张问善人之道。子曰:"不践迹,亦不入于
shì
室。"

21

先进第十一　Chapter Eleven

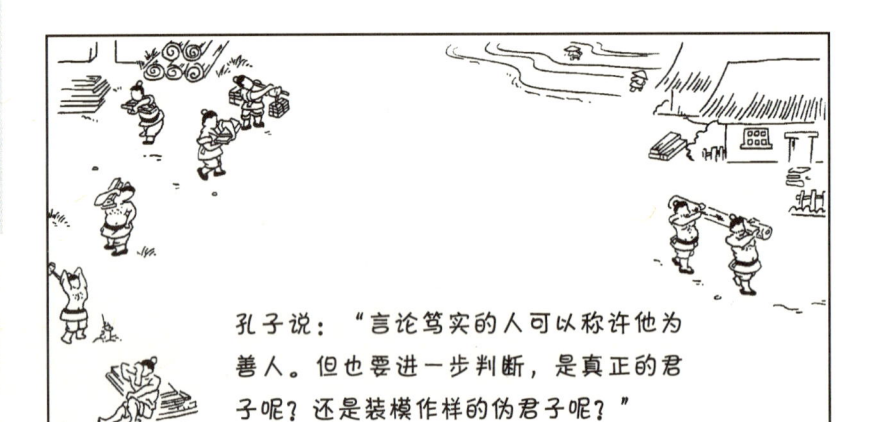

【释义】

孔子说:"言论笃实的人可以称许他为善人。但也要进一步判断,是真正的君子呢?还是装模作样的伪君子呢?"

【英译】

The Master said, "I praise people who speak sincerely, but I also make further judgment: is he really a man of virtue or a hypocrite?"

孔子说:"言论笃实的人可以称许他为善人。但也要进一步判断,是真正的君子呢?还是装模作样的伪君子呢?"

The Master said, "I praise people who speak sincerely, but I also make further judgment: is he really a man of virtue or a hypocrite?"

11.21
zǐ yuē　　　lùn dǔ shì yù　　jūn zǐ zhě hū　　sè zhuāng zhě hū
子曰:"论笃是与。君子者乎?色庄者乎?"

Chapter Eleven 先进第十一

孔子说:"冉求退缩不前,因此使他勇进;仲由好强争胜,因此使他谦让。"

The Master said, "Yan Qiu is timid, so I urged him on. Zhong You tends to be too bold, so I tried to hold him back."

11.22
zǐ lù wèn　　　　wén sī xíng zhū　　　zǐ yuē　　　yǒu fù xiōng zài
子路问:"闻斯行诸?"子曰:"有父兄在,
rú zhī hé qí wén sī xíng zhī
如之何其闻斯行之?"
rǎn yǒu wèn　　　wén sī xíng zhū　　　zǐ yuē　　wén sī xíng zhī
冉有问:"闻斯行诸?"子曰:"闻斯行之。"

【释义】

　　子路问道:"听到以后便去实践它吗?"孔子说:"有父兄在世,如何能不奉命行事,听到以后便去实践它呢?"

　　冉有问道:"听到以后便去实践它吗?"孔子说:"听到以后便去实践它。"

【英译】

　　Zi Lu asked, "When I have learned something, should I immediately put it into practice?" The Master answered, "Since your father and elder brothers are still alive, how can you practice what you have learned without consulting them first?"

　　Ran You asked, "When I have learned something, should I immediately put it into practice?" The Master answered, "Yes, practice what you have learned immediately after you have learned it."

先进第十一　Chapter Eleven

gōng xī huá yuē　　yóu yě wèn　wén sī xíng zhū　　zǐ yuē　　yǒu fù
公西华曰："由也问'闻斯行诸',子曰'有父
xiōng zài　　　qiú yě wèn　wén sī xíng zhū　　zǐ yuē　wén sī xíng
兄在';求也问'闻斯行诸',子曰'闻斯行
zhī　　chì yě huò　gǎn wèn　zǐ yuē　qiú yě tuì　gù jìn
之'。赤也惑,敢问。"子曰:"求也退,故进
zhī　yóu yě jiān rén　gù tuì zhī
之;由也兼人,故退之。"

【释义】

公西华说:"仲由问'听到以后便去实践它吗',先生说'有父兄在世';冉求问'听到以后便去实践它吗',先生说'听到以后便去实践它'。我疑惑不解,大胆冒昧地问问。"孔子说:"冉求退缩不前,因此使他勇进;仲由好强争胜,因此使他谦让。"

【英译】

Gongxi Hua felt puzzled and asked, "When Zhong You (Zi Lu) asked you whether he should immediately practice what he had learned, you told him that he should not do it, but when Ran Qiu (Ran You) asked you the same question, you told him that he should do it. May I venture to ask, why did you give different answers to the same question?" The Master explained, "Ran Qiu is timid, so I urged him on. Zhong You tends to be too bold, so I tried to hold him back."

Chapter Eleven 先进第十一

颜渊说："先生还在，我颜回怎敢轻易死呢？"

Yan Yuan said, "When you are alive, how would I dare to die?"

【释义】

孔子被拘禁在匡邑，颜渊落在后面。重逢时孔子说："我以为你死了呢。"颜渊说："先生还在，我颜回怎敢轻易死呢？"

【英译】

When the Master and his disciples were trapped in Kuang, Yan Yuan (Yan Hui) was the last one to escape. The Master said, "I thought you were dead." Yan Hui answered, "When you are alive, how would I dare to die?"

11.23
zǐ wèi yú kuāng　yán yuān hòu　zǐ yuē　wú yǐ rǔ wéi sǐ yǐ
子畏于匡，颜渊后。子曰："吾以女为死矣。"
yuē　zǐ zài　huí hé gǎn sǐ
曰："子在，回何敢死？"

先进第十一 Chapter Eleven

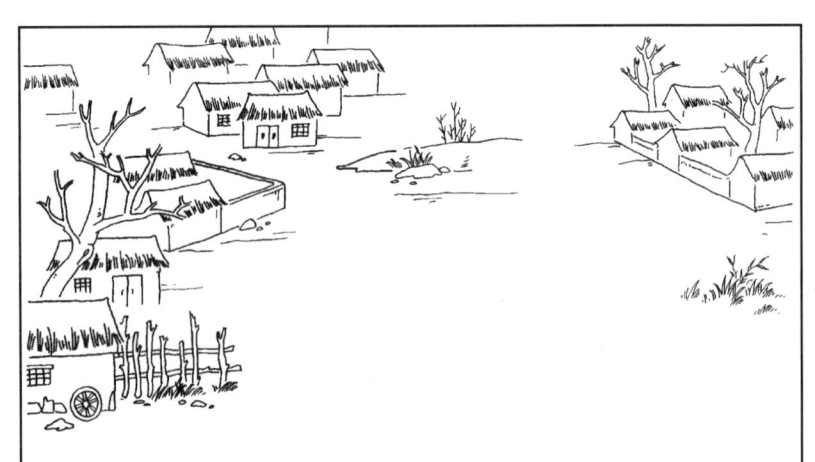

孔子说："如果君上让臣弑父弑君，也不会服从的。"

The Master said, "If they were told to murder their own father or the ruler, they would definitely not do it."

11.24
jì zǐ rán wèn   zhòng yóu rǎn qiú   kě wèi dà chén yú   zǐ
季子然问："仲由、冉求，可谓大臣与？"子
yuē   wú yǐ zǐ wéi yì zhī wèn   zēng yóu yǔ qiú zhī wèn   suǒ wèi
曰："吾以子为异之问，曾由与求之问。所谓
dà chén zhě   yǐ dào shì jūn   bù kě zé zhǐ   jīn yóu yǔ qiú yě
大臣者，以道事君，不可则止。今由与求也，
kě wèi jù chén yǐ   yuē   rán zé cóng zhī zhě yú   zǐ yuē
可谓具臣矣。"曰："然则从之者与？"子曰：
shì fù yǔ jūn   yì bù cóng yě
"弑父与君，亦不从也。"

【释义】

季子然问道："仲由、冉求可称为大臣吗？"孔子说："我以为您是在问别人呢，原来是问仲由和冉求啊。所谓大臣，是用道义事奉君主，不可谏阻，也就作罢。现今的仲由和冉求，可称为有才干的办事之臣了。"季子然又问："那么，他们是绝对服从君上的人吗？"孔子说："如果君上让臣弑父弑君，也不会服从的。"

【英译】

Ji Ziran asked, "Can Zhong You (Zi Lu) and Ran Qiu be called great ministers?" The Master said, "I thought you would ask about someone else. I didn't expect you would ask about them. A great minister refers to the one who serves the ruler in accordance with the Way. If he cannot do that, he resigns. Zhong You (Zi Lu) and Ran Qiu can be said as having the competence of ministers." Ji Ziran then asked, "Would they always do what they are told to do?" The Master answered, "If they were told to murder their own fathers or the ruler, they would definitely not do it."

Chapter Eleven 先进第十一

> 孔子对子路说:"由于你这般狡辩,我更厌恶那些巧嘴俐舌的人。"
>
> The Master said to Zi Lu, "It is for such remarks of yours that I hate people who indulge in sophistry."

11.25

zǐ lù shǐ zǐ gāo wéi bì zǎi　　zǐ yuē　　zéi fú rén zhī zǐ
子路使子羔为费宰。子曰:"贼夫人之子。"
zǐ lù yuē　　　yǒu mín rén yān　yǒu shè jì yān　hé bì dú shū
子路曰:"有民人焉,有社稷焉。何必读书,
rán hòu wéi xué　　zǐ yuē　　shì gù wù fú nìng zhě
然后为学?"子曰:"是故恶夫佞者。"

【释义】

子路让子羔做费邑的长官。孔子说:"这是坑害别人的儿子。"子路说:"有老百姓在那里可以治理,有土神谷神在那里可以祭祀。为什么一定去读书,然后才算学习呢?"孔子说:"由于你这般狡辩,我更厌恶那些巧嘴俐舌的人。"

【英译】

　　Zi Lu has appointed Zi Gao as head of Bi. The Master said, "You are doing harm to a father's son." Zi Lu said, "In Bi, there are people to be ruled, and there are altars for the God of Soil and the God of Grain. Why does a man have to read in order to be considered learned?" The Master said, "It is for such remarks of yours that I hate people who indulge in sophistry."

Note: The Master believed that the young man Zi Gao shouldn't be taken away from his study.

先进第十一　Chapter Eleven

孔子说："我赞同曾点的志向。"

The Master said, "I'm in favor of Zeng Dian's aspiration."

11.26
zǐ lù　zēng xī　rǎn yǒu　gōng xī huá shì zuò
子路、曾皙、冉有、公西华侍坐。
zǐ yuē　　 yǐ wú yí rì zhǎng hū ěr　 wú wú yǐ yě　 jū zé yuē
子曰："以吾一日长乎尔，毋吾以也。居则曰：
bù wú zhī yě　　 rú huò zhī ěr　 zé hé yǐ zāi
'不吾知也！'如或知尔，则何以哉？"
zǐ lù shuài ěr ér duì yuē　 qiān shèng zhī guó　 shè hū dà guó zhī jiān
子路率尔而对曰："千乘之国，摄乎大国之间，
jiā zhī yǐ shī lǚ　 yīn zhī yǐ jī jǐn　 yóu yě wéi zhī　 bǐ jí sān
加之以师旅，因之以饥馑，由也为之，比及三
nián　 kě shǐ yǒu yǒng　 qiě zhī fāng yě
年，可使有勇，且知方也。"

【释义】

　　子路、曾皙、冉有、公西华陪坐在孔子身旁。

　　孔子说："因为我比你们年长一些，不要因为我而拘束。你们平常总是说：'不了解我啊！'如果有人了解你们，那么你们将怎样做呢？"

　　子路急忙回答说："拥有一千辆兵车的国家，局促地处在大国中间，外面受到军事进犯，里面发生灾情饥荒，我来治理它，等到三年，可使民众勇敢有力，并且明白道义。"

【英译】

　　Once, with Zi Lu, Zeng Xi (Zeng Dian), Ran You (Ran Qiu) and Gongxi Hua (Gongxi Chi) attending him, the Master said, "Don't feel restrained simply because I'm your senior in age. You often say, 'My competence is not recognized.' Now if someone did recognize your competence and were willing to employ you, what would you do?"

　　Zi Lu answered immediately, "If I were to govern a state with one thousand war chariots that were situated between powerful neighbors and were suffering famine and foreign military threat, I could, in three years' time, make the people brave and respectful of the rituals."

Chapter Eleven 先进第十一

夫子哂之。"求，尔何如？"对曰："方六七十，如五六十，求也为之，比及三年，可使足民。如其礼乐，以俟君子。"

"赤，尔何如？"对曰："非曰能之，愿学焉。宗庙之事，如会同，端章甫，愿为小相焉。"

【释义】

孔子微微一笑。又问："冉求，你怎么样？"冉求回答说："疆土纵横六七十里，或者纵横五六十里的小国，我来治理它，等到三年，可使民众富足。至于礼乐教化，有待君子推行了。"

又问："公西赤，你怎么样？"公西华回答说："不敢说能干什么，愿意学习。宗庙祭祀之事，或者外交会见仪式，自己穿戴好礼服礼帽，愿做一个小司仪。"

【英译】

The Master smiled, and then asked, "What about you, Ran Qiu?" Ran Qiu answered, "If I were to govern a small state of sixty to seventy or fifty to sixty square *li*, I could, in three years' time, make the people rich. As for rituals and music, I leave them to men of virtue."

The Master turned to Gongxi Chi and asked, "What about you?" Gongxi Hua answered, "I dare not say what I could do, but I'm ready to learn. I would be willing to dress up in ceremonial clothes and hat and work as a minor master of ceremonies on occasions of offering sacrifice at ancestral temples or meeting with foreign guests."

先进第十一 Chapter Eleven

"点，尔何如？"鼓瑟希，铿尔，舍瑟而作，对曰："异乎三子者之撰。"子曰："何伤乎？亦各言其志也。"曰："莫春者，春服既成，冠者五六人，童子六七人，浴乎沂，风乎舞雩，咏而归。"夫子喟然叹曰："吾与点也。"

【释义】

又问："曾点，你怎么样？"曾皙正在弹瑟，瑟声渐渐稀落，"铿"的一声，放下瑟站起来，回答说："我的志向不同于前面三位讲的。"孔子说："有什么妨碍呢？也不过是各自谈谈自己的志向。"曾皙说："暮春时节，春服已经换上，约上五六个青年，六七个少年，在沂水里洗洗澡，在舞雩坛上吹吹风，然后唱着歌归来。"孔子长长叹了一声说："我赞同曾点的志向。"

【英译】

The Master turned to Zeng Dian and asked, "And you, Zeng Dian?" Zeng Xi was playing the *se*. He finished the last notes and said, "I have different aspirations from the three of them." The Master said, "That's all right. What's the harm in telling us your aspirations?" Zeng Xi answered, "In late spring, I would put on my spring clothes and go to bathe in the Yi River with five or six young adults and six or seven boys. Afterwards we would enjoy the breeze on the Wuyu Altar and then sing all our way home." The Master said with a deep sigh, "I'm in favor of Zeng Dian's aspiration."

Chapter Eleven 先进第十一

三子者出，曾皙后。曾皙曰："夫三子者之言何如？"子曰："亦各言其志也已矣。"曰："夫子何哂由也？"曰："为国以礼，其言不让，是故哂之。唯求则非邦也与？安见方六七十如五六十而非邦也者？唯赤则非邦也与？"

【释义】

子路、冉有、公西华三人出去了，曾皙留在最后。曾皙向孔子问道："他们三人的话怎么样？"孔子说："也不过是各自谈谈自己的志向罢了。"曾皙问："先生为什么笑仲由呢？"孔子说："治理国家靠的是礼让，他出言一点儿也不谦让，所以笑他。难道冉求讲的就不是治理国家的事吗？怎见得疆土纵横六七十里或者五六十里不是国家呢？难道公西赤讲的就不是治理国家的事吗？"

【英译】

After Zi Lu, Ran You and Gongxi Hua had left, Zeng Xi stayed behind and asked, "What do you think of the answers of the three of them?" The Master said, "They are nothing but their aspirations." Zeng Xi asked, "Why did you smile at Zi Lu?" The Master answered, "The governing of a state involves respect and courtesy on the part of the ruler. What he said didn't show any modesty. That's why I smiled at him. What Ran Qiu said also referred to the governing of a state, am I right? Is an area of sixty to seventy or fifty to sixty square *li* big enough to be called a state? What Gongxi Chi said was also related to the affairs of a state, right?"

先进第十一　Chapter Eleven

"宗庙会同，非诸侯而何？赤也为之小，孰能为之大？"

【释义】

"宗庙祭祀，外交会见，不是诸侯国的事又是什么？公西赤如做一个国家的小司仪，谁还能做一个国家的大司仪呢？"

【英译】

"Surely offering sacrifice at ancestral temples and meeting with foreign guests are part of state affairs. If Gongxi Chi were only qualified for a minor master of ceremonies, who would be qualified for a major master of ceremonies?"

yán yuān dì shí èr
颜渊第十二
CHAPTER TWELVE

颜渊第十二　Chapter Twelve

孔子说："约束自己照着礼的要求去做，就是仁。"

The Master said, "To restrain oneself and act in accord with etiquette, this is benevolence."

【释义】

颜渊问什么是仁。孔子说："约束自己照着礼的要求去做，就是仁。一旦做到了这一点，天下就都归于仁了。实行仁德全在于自己，还能靠别人吗？"颜渊说："请问修养仁德的具体细节。"孔子说："不符合礼的事不看，不符合礼的话不听，不符合礼的话不说，不符合礼的事不做。"颜渊说："我虽然不聪敏，请让我按照这话努力去做吧。"

【英译】

Yan Yuan asked about benevolence. The Master answered, "To restrain oneself and act in accord with etiquette is benevolence; once everyone restrains themselves and submits to etiquette, the whole world will enjoy virtue. Benevolence is pursued out of one's own desire, it can not be forced upon by others." Yan Yuan asked about specific details to achieve benevolence. The Master said, "Do not look at things in defiance of etiquette, do not listen to things in defiance of etiquette, do not say things in defiance of etiquette, and do not do things in defiance of etiquette." Yan Yuan said, "Although I am not intelligent, I will act according to your instructions."

12.1 颜渊问仁。子曰："克己复礼为仁。一日克己复礼，天下归仁焉。为仁由己，而由人乎哉？"颜渊曰："请问其目。"子曰："非礼勿视，非礼勿听，非礼勿言，非礼勿动。"颜渊曰："回虽不敏，请事斯语矣。"

Chapter Twelve　颜渊第十二

孔子说："自己不愿承受的事物，不要加给别人。"

The Master said, "Do not do to others what you would not like to be done to you."

12.2
仲弓问仁。子曰："出门如见大宾，使民如承大祭。己所不欲，勿施于人。在邦无怨，在家无怨。"仲弓曰："雍虽不敏，请事斯语矣。"

【释义】

仲弓问什么是仁。孔子说："出门在外要像接见贵宾一样敬慎，役使老百姓要像承当大的祭典一样小心。自己不愿承受的事物，不要加给别人。在诸侯之国做官不招致怨恨，在大夫之家做官也不招致怨恨。"仲弓说："我虽然不聪敏，请让我按照这话努力去做吧。"

【英译】

Zhong Gong asked about benevolence. The Master said, "When away from home, behave in a way as if you were in the presence of a distinguished guest. And when ordering people to do things, treat them in a way as if you were holding an important ceremony of sacrifice. Do not do to others what you would not like to be done to you. Then no one will bear grudges against you, whether you hold office in the government or stay at home." Zhong Gong said, "Although I am not intelligent, I will act according to your instructions."

颜渊第十二　Chapter Twelve

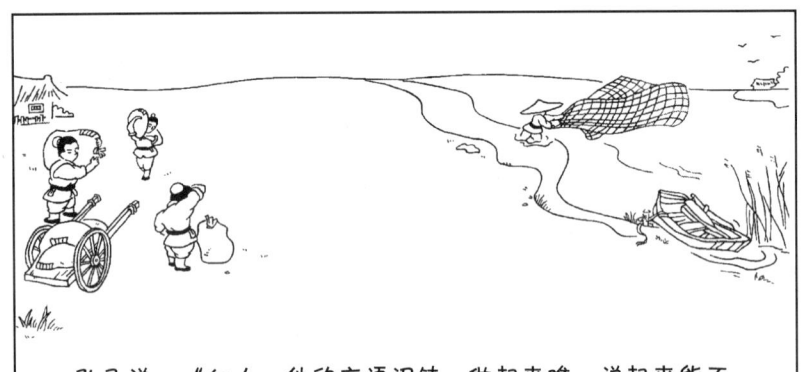

孔子说："仁人，他的言语迟钝。做起来难，说起来能不迟钝吗？"

The Master said, "A benevolent man speaks very cautiously. Since it is hard to put words into action, how can one afford not to speak cautiously?"

12.3
sī mǎ niú wèn rén   zǐ yuē   rén zhě   qí yán yě rèn
司马牛问仁。子曰："仁者，其言也讱。"
yuē   qí yán yě rèn   sī wèi zhī rén yǐ hū   zǐ yuē
曰："其言也讱，斯谓之仁已乎？"子曰：
wéi zhī nán   yán zhī dé wú rèn hū
"为之难，言之得无讱乎？"

【释义】

司马牛问什么是仁。孔子说："仁人，他的言语迟钝。"

司马牛又问："言语迟钝，这就能叫做仁了吗？"孔子说："做起来难，说起来能不迟钝吗？"

【英译】

Sima Niu asked about benevolence. The Master said, "A benevolent man speaks very cautiously."

Sima Niu asked again, "Does this mean a man who speaks cautiously can be considered as benevolent?" The Master answered, "Since it is hard to put words into action, how can one afford not to speak cautiously?"

Chapter Twelve 颜渊第十二

孔子说:"君子不忧愁,不恐惧。"

The Master said, "A man of virtue is neither worried nor afraid."

12.4
sī mǎ niú wèn jūn zǐ　　zǐ yuē　　　jūn zǐ bù yōu bú jù
司马牛问君子。子曰:"君子不忧不惧。"
yuē　　bù yōu bú jù　　sī wèi zhī jūn zǐ yǐ hū　　zǐ yuē
曰:"不忧不惧,斯谓之君子已乎?"子曰:
nèi xǐng bú jiù　　fú hé yōu hé jù
"内省不疚,夫何忧何惧?"

【释义】

　　司马牛问什么是君子。孔子说:"君子不忧愁,不恐惧。"

　　又问:"不忧愁,不恐惧,这就能叫做君子了吗?"孔子说:"内心反省不感到有错而悔恨,那又愁什么,怕什么呢?"

【英译】

　　Sima Niu asked about how to be a man of virtue. The Master answered, "A man of virtue is neither worried nor afraid."

　　Sima Niu then asked, "Does this mean a man who is neither worried nor afraid can be called a man of virtue?" The Master answered, "With a clear conscience, what is there to be worried or afraid of?"

颜渊第十二　Chapter Twelve

子夏说："君子何愁没有兄弟呢？"

Zi Xia said, "How can a man of virtue complain about not having brothers?"

12.5
sī mǎ niú yōu yuē　　　　rén jiē yǒu xiōng dì　　wǒ dú wú　　zǐ xià
司马牛忧曰："人皆有兄弟，我独亡。"子夏
yuē　　shāng wén zhī yǐ　　　sǐ shēng yǒu mìng　fù guì zài tiān
曰："商闻之矣：'死生有命，富贵在天。'
jūn zǐ jìng ér wú shī　　yǔ rén gōng ér yǒu lǐ　　sì hǎi zhī nèi　　jiē
君子敬而无失，与人恭而有礼，四海之内，皆
xiōng dì yě　　jūn zǐ hé huàn hū wú xiōng dì yě
兄弟也。君子何患乎无兄弟也？'"

【释义】

司马牛忧愁地说："别人都有兄弟，唯独我没有。"子夏说："我听说过：'死生有命，富贵在天。'君子只要严肃认真地对待所做的事情，不出差错，对人恭敬而合乎礼的规定，那么，天下人就都是自己的兄弟了。君子何愁没有兄弟呢？"

【英译】

Sima Niu lamented, "Everyone else has brothers. How come I alone do not?" Zi Xia replied, "I have heard that death and life are controlled by Heaven, and wealth and rank hinge on the will of Heaven, too. But if a man behaves with courtesy to others and conforms to etiquette, he will surely have brothers all over the world. So how can a man of virtue complain about not having brothers?"

Chapter Twelve 颜渊第十二

孔子说:"像水的浸润那样点滴积累的谗言和像有切肤之痛那样急迫切身的诽谤,在他面前都行不通,那就可以说是明智了。"

The Master said, "A man who does not buy assiduous slanders or brazen libels can be regarded as clear-sighted. Such a man can also be called far-sighted."

12.6

zǐ zhāng wèn míng。zǐ yuē:"jìn rùn zhī zèn,fū shòu zhī sù,bù
子张问明。子曰:"浸润之谮,肤受之愬,不
xíng yān,kě wèi míng yě yǐ yǐ。jìn rùn zhī zèn,fū shòu zhī sù,
行焉,可谓明也已矣。浸润之谮,肤受之愬,
bù xíng yān,kě wèi yuǎn yě yǐ yǐ。"
不行焉,可谓远也已矣。"

【释义】

子张问怎样才是明察。孔子说:"像水的浸润那样点滴积累的谗言和像有切肤之痛那样急迫切身的诽谤,在他面前都行不通,那就可以说是明智了。像水的浸润那样点滴积累的谗言和像有切肤之痛急迫切身的诽谤,在他面前都行不通,那就可以说是很有远见了。"

【英译】

Zi Zhang asked about clear-sightedness. The Master said, "A man who does not buy assiduous slanders or brazen libels can be regarded as clear-sighted. Such a man can also be called far-sighted."

颜渊第十二　Chapter Twelve

【释义】

子贡问为政之道。孔子说："备足粮食，充实军备，取信于民。"子贡说："如果迫不得已要去掉一方面，在粮食、军备、民信这三方面中先去掉哪一方面？"孔子说："去掉军备。"子贡说："如果迫不得已还要去掉一方面，在剩下的两方面中先去掉哪一方面？"孔子说："去掉粮食。自古以来谁都难免于死，无粮顶多饿死，如果老百姓没有对政府的信任，国家根本站不住。"

【英译】

Zi Gong asked about the elements of successful government. The Master answered, "Sufficient food, sufficient weapons, and trust of the people." Zi Gong asked further, "If among these three, one had to be discarded, what would that be?" The Master answered, "Weapons." Zi Gong then asked, "If among the two left, one had to be discarded, what would that be?" The Master answered, "Food. Since ancient times till now all people have to die, but if a government lost the trust of its people, then it would not be able to sustain itself."

12.7

zǐ gòng wèn zhèng　zǐ yuē　　zú shí　zú bīng　mín xìn zhī yǐ
子贡问政。子曰："足食，足兵，民信之矣。"
zǐ gòng yuē　　bì bù dé yǐ ér qù　　yú sī sān zhě hé xiān
子贡曰："必不得已而去，于斯三者何先？"
yuē　　qù bīng　　zǐ gòng yuē　　bì bù dé yǐ ér qù　yú
曰："去兵。"子贡曰："必不得已而去，于
sī èr zhě hé xiān　　yuē　　qù shí　zì gǔ jiē yǒu sǐ　mín
斯二者何先？"曰："去食。自古皆有死，民
wú xìn bú lì
无信不立。"

Chapter Twelve 颜渊第十二

子贡说："本质如同文饰一样重要。"

Zi Gong said, "Qualities and refinement are interdependent and they are of equal importance."

12.8
jí zǐ chéng yuē jūn zǐ zhì ér yǐ yǐ hé yǐ wén wéi zǐ
棘子成曰："君子质而已矣，何以文为？"子
gòng yuē xī hū fū zǐ zhī shuō jūn zǐ yě sì bù jí shé
贡曰："惜乎，夫子之说君子也！驷不及舌。
wén yóu zhì yě zhì yóu wén yě hǔ bào zhī kuò yóu quǎn yáng zhī kuò
文犹质也，质犹文也。虎豹之鞟犹犬羊之鞟。"

【释义】

棘子成说："君子有其美质也就罢了，要文饰又有什么用呢？"子贡说："可惜啊，先生你竟这样来解说君子！一言出口，驷马难追。文饰如同本质一样重要，本质如同文饰一样重要。如果去掉毛色花纹，虎豹的皮就和犬羊的皮没有区别了。"

【英译】

Ji Zicheng said, "For a man of virtue, noble qualities are enough. What's the use of cultural refinement?" Zi Gong said, "It is a pity that you talk about a man of virtue this way! Once the words are said, they can't be pulled back even by the force of a team of four horses. Qualities and refinement are interdependent and they are of equal importance. Without the colored fur, the skin of a tiger or leopard would be of no difference from that of a dog or sheep."

41

颜渊第十二　Chapter Twelve

> 有若说："百姓富足了，君上怎么会不富足呢？百姓贫困，用度不够，君上又怎么会富足呢？"

You Ruo said, "When the common people are affluent, how can you be left in need? In the same sense, when the common people are in need, how can you be affluent?"

12.9
āi gōng wèn yú yǒu ruò yuē　nián jī　yòng bù zú　rú zhī hé
哀公问于有若曰："年饥，用不足，如之何？"
yǒu ruò duì yuē　　hé chè hū　　yuē　　èr　wú yóu bù zú
有若对曰："盍彻乎？"曰："二，吾犹不足，
rú zhī hé qí chè yě　　duì yuē　　bǎi xìng zú　jūn shú yǔ bù
如之何其彻也？"对曰："百姓足，君孰与不
zú　bǎi xìng bù zú　　jūn shú yǔ zú
足？百姓不足，君孰与足？"

【释义】

哀公向有若问道："年景饥荒，用度不足，怎么办？"有若答道："为什么不用十分抽一的彻法呢？"哀公说："十分抽二，我还感到不足，怎么能用十分抽一的彻法呢？"有若答道："百姓富足了，君上怎么会不富足呢？百姓贫困，用度不够，君上又怎么会富足呢？"

【英译】

Duke Ai of the State of Lu asked You Ruo, "The grain yield is low, and I do not have enough to cover the expenditures. What shall I do?" You Ruo answered, "Why not adjust the land tax to one-tenth of the yield?" Duke Ai said, "Now I collect a land tax of two-tenths, and yet I do not have enough to cover the expenditures. How can I possibly lower it to one-tenth?" You Ruo answered, "When the common people are affluent, how can you be left in need? In the same sense, when the common people are in need, how can you be affluent?"

Chapter Twelve 颜渊第十二

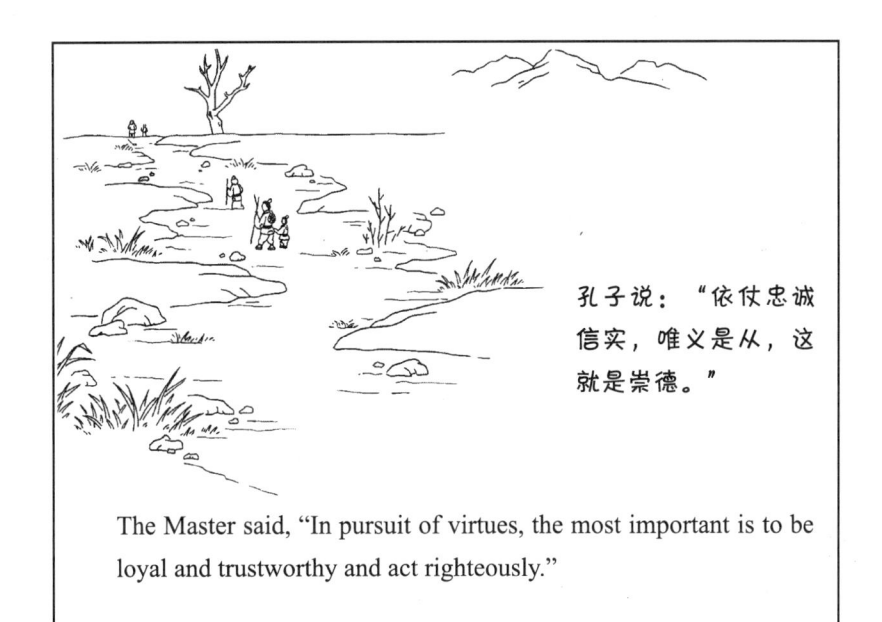

孔子说:"依仗忠诚信实,唯义是从,这就是崇德。"

The Master said, "In pursuit of virtues, the most important is to be loyal and trustworthy and act righteously."

12.10
zǐ zhāng wèn chóng dé　biàn huò　zǐ yuē　zhǔ zhōng xìn　xǐ yì
子 张 问 崇 德、辨 惑。子 曰:"主 忠 信,徙 义,
chóng dé yě　ài zhī yù qí shēng　wù zhī yù qí sǐ　jì yù qí shēng
崇 德 也。爱 之 欲 其 生,恶 之 欲 其 死。既 欲 其 生,
yòu yù qí sǐ　shì huò yě　chéng bù yǐ fù　yì zhǐ yǐ yì
又 欲 其 死,是 惑 也。'诚 不 以 富,亦 祇 以 异。'"

【释义】

子张问什么是崇德、辨惑。孔子说:"依仗忠诚信实,唯义是从,这就是崇德。喜爱一个人便想要他活,厌恶一个人便想要他死。既想要他活,又想要他死,这就是疑惑。这正如《诗经》所说:'诚然不足以致富,而恰恰足以生异。'"

【英译】

Zi Zhang asked about pursuit of virtues and avoidance of confusion. The Master answered, "In pursuit of virtues, the most important is to be loyal and trustworthy and act righteously. If you love a man, you want him to live well; if you hate a man, you want him to die. To both want a man to live and die at the same time is confusion. As *The Book of Songs* says, 'If not for the wealth, then it must be for a change.'"

颜渊第十二　Chapter Twelve

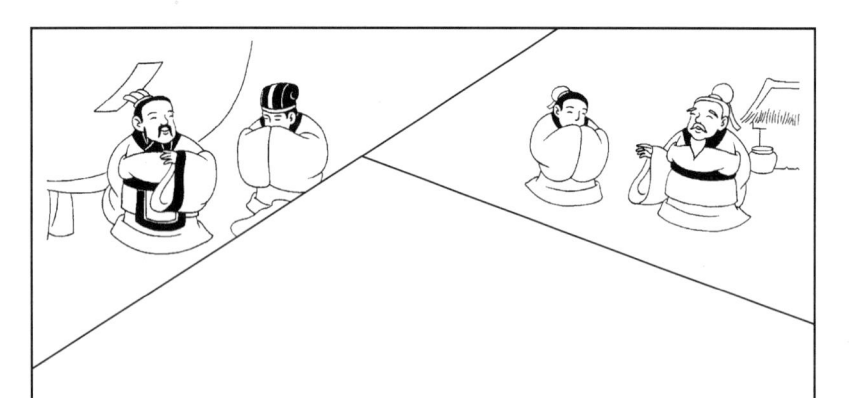

孔子说："君尽君道，臣尽臣道，父尽父道，子尽子道。"

The Master said, "Let the ruler be a ruler, the subject a subject, the father a father, the son a son."

12.11
qí jǐng gōng wèn zhèng yú kǒng zǐ　kǒng zǐ duì yuē　　jūn jūn chén
齐景公问政于孔子。孔子对曰："君君，臣
chén　fù fù　zǐ zǐ　　gōng yuē　shàn zāi　xìn rú jūn bù
臣，父父，子子。"公曰："善哉！信如君不
jūn　chén bù chén　fù bú fù　zǐ bù zǐ　suī yǒu sù　wú dé
君，臣不臣，父不父，子不子，虽有粟，吾得
ér shí zhū
而食诸？"

【释义】

齐景公向孔子问为政之道。孔子答道："君尽君道，臣尽臣道，父尽父道，子尽子道。"景公说："好极了！诚然，如果君不尽君道，臣不尽臣道，父不尽父道，子不尽子道，即使有粮食储备，我能吃得着吗？"

【英译】

Duke Jing of the State of Qi asked about the way of government. The Master said, "Let the ruler be a ruler, the subject a subject, the father a father, the son a son." Duke Jing said, "Great! If the ruler did not act like a ruler, the subject not a subject, the father not a father and the son not a son, even if there were grain, would I get my share?"

Chapter Twelve 颜渊第十二

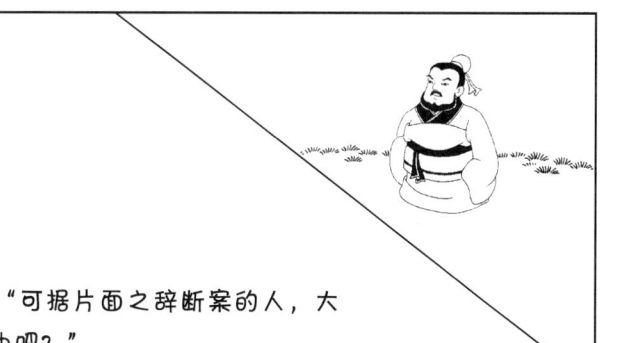

孔子说:"可据片面之辞断案的人,大概就是仲由吧?"

The Master said, "Zhong You (Zi Lu) is probably the man who can settle a litigation case by listening to only one side."

【释义】

孔子说:"可据片面之辞断案的人,大概就是仲由吧。"子路没有拖延未兑现的诺言。

【英译】

The Master said, "Zhong You (Zi Lu) is probably the man who can settle a litigation case by listening to only one side." Zi Lu always fulfilled his promises shortly after he had made them.

12.12
zǐ yuē　　　piàn yán kě yǐ zhé yù zhě　　qí yóu yě yú　　　zǐ lù
子曰:"片言可以折狱者,其由也与!"子路
wú sù nuò
无宿诺。

45

颜渊第十二　Chapter Twelve

孔子说："审理诉讼案件，我同别人是一样的。重要的是一定要做到没有诉讼案件才好。"

The Master said, "In dealing with lawsuits, I am no different from others. We wish there would be no more lawsuits."

【释义】

孔子说："审理诉讼案件，我同别人是一样的。重要的是一定要做到没有诉讼案件才好。"

【英译】

The Master said, "In dealing with lawsuits, I am no different from others. We wish there would be no more lawsuits."

12.13
zǐ yuē　　　tīng sòng　　wú yóu rén yě　　bì yě shǐ wú sòng hū
子曰："听讼，吾犹人也。必也使无讼乎！"

Chapter Twelve　颜渊第十二

孔子说："在位尽职不要倦怠，
执行政令要忠诚。"

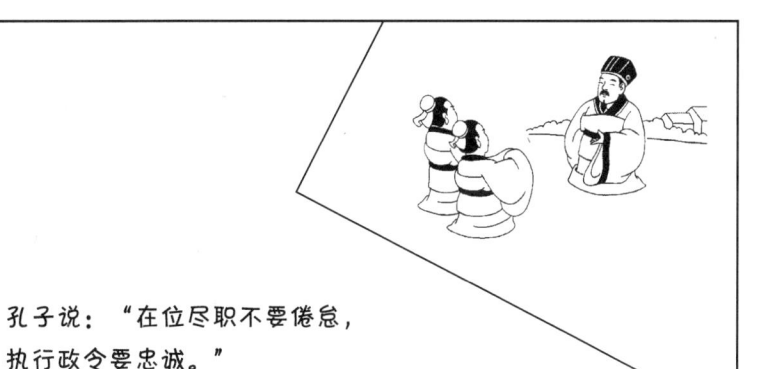

The Master said, "Work conscientiously in your position, and remain loyal in carrying out government orders."

【释义】

　　子张问为政之道。孔子说："在位尽职不要倦怠，执行政令要忠诚。"

【英译】

　　Zi Zhang asked about the way of government. The Master answered, "Work conscientiously in your position, and remain loyal in carrying out government orders."

12.14 zǐ zhāng wèn zhèng　zǐ yuē　　jū zhī wú juàn　xíng zhī yǐ zhōng
子张问政。子曰："居之无倦，行之以忠。"

颜渊第十二　Chapter Twelve

【释义】

孔子说:"君子广泛地学习文化知识,并且用礼来约束自己,也就可以不离经叛道了啊!"

【英译】

The Master said, "Acquire broad knowledge and restrain yourself with etiquette. Thus you won't go against the way of a man of virtue."

孔子说:"君子广泛地学习文化知识,并且用礼来约束自己,也就可以不离经叛道了啊!"

The Master said, "Acquire broad knowledge and restrain yourself with etiquette. Thus you won't go against the way of a man of virtue."

12.15

zǐ yuē　　　　bó xué yú wén　　yuē zhī yǐ lǐ　　yì kě yǐ fú pàn
子曰:"博学于文,约之以礼,亦可以弗畔

yǐ fú
矣夫!"

Chapter Twelve 颜渊第十二

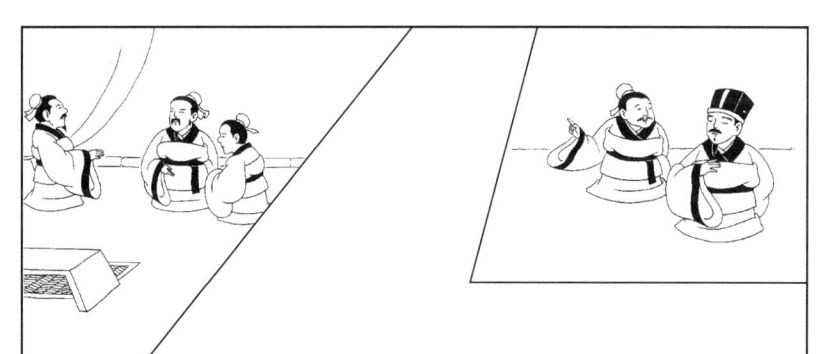

孔子说："君子成全别人的好事，而不促成别人的坏事。小人则与此相反。"

The Master said, "A man of virtue always tries to facilitate the accomplishment of others. He never helps others do evil acts. A petty-minded man is just the opposite."

【释义】

孔子说："君子成全别人的好事，而不促成别人的坏事。小人则与此相反。"

【英译】

The Master said, "A man of virtue always tries to facilitate the accomplishment of others. He never helps others do evil acts. A petty-minded man is just the opposite."

12.16

zǐ yuē　　jūn zǐ chéng rén zhī měi　　bù chéng rén zhī è　　xiǎo rén fǎn
子曰："君子成人之美，不成人之恶。小人反
shì
是。"

孔子对季康子说:"政字的意思就是端正。您自己带头端正行为,谁敢不端正行为呢?"

The Master said to Ji Kangzi, "Governing is straightening. If you take the lead in being righteous, who dare do the opposite?"

【释义】

季康子向孔子问为政之道。孔子回答说:"政字的意思就是端正。您自己带头端正行为,谁敢不端正行为呢?"

【英译】

Ji Kangzi asked about the way of government. The Master replied, "Governing is straightening. If you take the lead in being righteous, who dare do the opposite?"

12.17
jì kāng zǐ wèn zhèng yú kǒng zǐ　kǒng zǐ duì yuē　zhèng zhě zhèng
季康子问政于孔子。孔子对曰:"政者,正
yě　zǐ shuài yǐ zhèng　shú gǎn bú zhèng
也。子帅以正,孰敢不正?"

Chapter Twelve 颜渊第十二

【释义】

季康子苦于盗贼的扰乱，向孔子询问对策。孔子说："假如你不贪求财物，即使奖励他们盗窃，他们也不会盗窃。"

【英译】

Ji Kangzi consulted the Master on ways to get rid of theft in the state. The Master said, "If you were free from unreasonable desires for personal gain, then the common people would not steal even if they would be awarded for doing so."

The Master said to Ji Kangzi, "If you were free from unreasonable desires for personal gain, then the common people would not steal even if they would be awarded for doing so."

12.18

jì kāng zǐ huàn dào　　wèn yú kǒng zǐ　　kǒng zǐ duì yuē　　gǒu zǐ zhī
季康子患盗，问于孔子。孔子对曰："苟子之
bú yù　　suī shǎng zhī bú qiè
不欲，虽赏之不窃。"

颜渊第十二 Chapter Twelve

孔子对季康子说:"您要好从善,那么老百姓也就会好从善了。"

The Master said to Ji Kangzi, "If you take the lead in doing what is right, then the common people will follow you in doing what is right."

12.19
jì kāng zǐ wèn zhèng yú kǒng zǐ yuē rú shā wú dào yǐ jiù yǒu
季康子问政于孔子曰:"如杀无道,以就有
dào hé rú   kǒng zǐ duì yuē   zǐ wéi zhèng yān yòng shā
道,何如?"孔子对曰:"子为政,焉用杀?
zǐ yù shàn ér mín shàn yǐ jūn zǐ zhī dé fēng xiǎo rén zhī dé
子欲善,而民善矣。君子之德风,小人之德
cǎo cǎo shàng zhī fēng bì yǎn
草,草上之风,必偃。"

【释义】

季康子向孔子问为政之道,说:"如果杀掉无德无才的坏人,来亲近有德有才的好人,怎么样?"孔子答道:"您治理国政,何必用杀戮?您要好从善,那么老百姓也就会好从善了。君子的道德好比风,小人的道德好比草,草受到风,一定随风倒伏。"

【英译】

Ji Kangzi asked about the way of government, "What do you think of killing evil people and getting close to good people?" The Master answered, "In governing a state, what's the point in killing people? If you take the lead in doing what is right, then the common people will follow you in doing what is right. The quality of a man of virtue is like wind while that of a petty-minded man is like grass. The wind blows on top, and the grass will surely bend under the wind."

Chapter Twelve 颜渊第十二

孔子说："至于达，品质正直，喜好大义，察其言语观其容色，又总是自觉谦让于人。"

The Master said, "A man of accomplishments is upright and always acts in accordance with etiquette. He is sensitive to others' words and observant of others' facial expressions. He is also considerate and courteous to other people."

12.20 子张问："士何如斯可谓之达矣？"子曰："何哉，尔所谓达者？"子张对曰："在邦必闻，在家必闻。"子曰："是闻也，非达也。"

【释义】

子张问道："士怎样才可称得上达呢？"孔子说："你所说的达是什么意思？"子张回答道："在诸侯之国做官一定有名望，在大夫之家做官也一定有名望。"孔子说："这是闻，不是达。"

【英译】

Zi Zhang asked, "What must a scholar do in order to be called accomplished?" The Master asked back, "What do you mean by 'accomplished'?", Zi Zhang answered, "To be renowned at both the ruler's court and his own clan." The Master said, "Being renowned does not equal being accomplished."

53

颜渊第十二 Chapter Twelve

"夫达也者，质直而好义，察言而观色，虑以下人。在邦必达，在家必达。夫闻也者，色取仁而行违，居之不疑。在邦必闻，在家必闻。"

【释义】

"至于达，品质正直，喜好大义，察其言语观其容色，又总是自觉谦让于人。那么，在诸侯之国做官一定通达，在大夫之家做官也一定通达。至于闻，表面上装出有仁德的样子，实际行动却违背仁德，还以仁人自居而从不怀疑自己。那么，在诸侯之国做官一定会骗取虚名，在大夫之家做官也一定会骗取虚名。"

【英译】

"A man of accomplishments is upright and always acts in accordance with etiquette. He is sensitive to others' words and observant of others' facial expressions. He is also considerate and courteous to other people. Such a man can achieve accomplishments both at the ruler's court and in his own clan. In contrast, a renowned man professes benevolence and acts against it. He does not feel ashamed for professing benevolence. Such a man may also be renowned at a ruler's court and in his own clan."

Chapter Twelve 颜渊第十二

孔子说:"先去做,然后有所收获,不是崇尚道德的方法吗?"

The Master said, "To think of work before reward is to exalt virtue."

12.21 fán chí cóng yóu yú wǔ yú zhī xià   yuē   gǎn wèn chóng dé   xiū tè
樊迟从游于舞雩之下,曰:"敢问崇德、修慝、
biàn huò   zǐ yuē   shàn zāi wèn   xiān shì hòu dé   fēi chóng dé
辨惑。"子曰:"善哉问!先事后得,非崇德
yú   gōng qí è   wú gōng rén zhī è   fēi xiū tè yú   yì zhāo zhī
与?攻其恶,无攻人之恶,非修慝与?一朝之
fèn   wàng qí shēn yǐ   jí qí qīn   fēi huò yú
忿,忘其身以及其亲,非惑与?"

【释义】

樊迟陪从孔子在舞雩台下闲游,说:"敢问怎样崇尚道德,整治过错,辨明迷惑?"孔子说:"问得好啊!先去做,然后有所收获,不是崇尚道德的方法吗?批判自己的过错,不去批判别人的过错,不是整治过错的方法吗?由于一时的忿怒,忘掉自身的安危得失,甚至连累自己的父母,不是执迷不悟吗?"

【英译】

When going on an outing with the Master near the Wuyu Altar, Fan Chi said, "May I venture to ask how to exalt virtue, eradicate evil and be clear-sighted?" The Master said, "What a good question! To think of work before reward is to exalt virtue; to exercise self-criticism instead of putting the blame on others is a way to eradicate evil; to act out of a sudden fit of anger without considering one's own safety and one's parents is a sign of being confused."

颜渊第十二　Chapter Twelve

孔子说："选拔正直之人，把他们放在歪邪之人的地位之上，能使歪邪之人正直起来。"

The Master said, "Select upright people and place them above crooked ones, thus the crooked will be made upright."

12.22
fán chí wèn rén　　zǐ yuē　　　　ài rén　　　wèn zhì　　zǐ yuē
樊迟问仁。子曰："爱人。"问知，子曰：
zhī rén
"知人。"
fán chí wèi dá　　zǐ yuē　　jǔ zhí cuò zhū wǎng　néng shǐ wǎng zhě zhí
樊迟未达。子曰："举直错诸枉，能使枉者直。"

【释义】

樊迟问什么是仁。孔子说："爱人。"又问什么是智，孔子说："知人。"

樊迟不明白是什么意思。孔子说："选拔正直之人，把他们放在歪邪之人的地位之上，能使歪邪之人正直起来。"

【英译】

Fan Chi asked about benevolence. The Master said, "Love people." Fan Chi then asked about wisdom. The Master said, "Understand people."

Fan did not get the meaning. The Master explained, "Select upright people and place them above crooked ones, thus the crooked will be made upright."

Chapter Twelve 颜渊第十二

樊迟退，见子夏，曰："向也吾见于夫子而问知，子曰：'举直错诸枉，能使枉者直。'何谓也？"

子夏曰："富哉言乎！舜有天下，选于众，举皋陶，不仁者远矣。汤有天下，选于众，举伊尹，不仁者远矣。"

【释义】

樊迟退下以后，见到子夏，说："刚才我见到先生，询问什么是智，先生说：'选拔正直之人，把他们放在歪邪之人的地位之上，能使歪邪之人正直起来。'这话是什么意思？"

子夏说："这话多么富有寓意呀！舜得了天下，在众人中选拔人才，举用皋陶，不仁的人纷纷远离而去。汤得了天下，在众人中选拔人才，举用伊尹，不仁的人纷纷远离而去。"

【英译】

Fan Chi came out of the Master's room and asked Zi Xia, "Just now, I went to see the Master and asked about wisdom. The Master said, 'Select upright people and place them above the crooked ones, thus the crooked will be made righteous.' What did he mean?"

Zi Xia said, "How rich in meaning his words are! When Emperor Shun was in reign, he selected Gao Tao from the multitude and promoted him, thus the unrighteous were kept away. When Tang was in reign, he selected Yi Yin from the multitude and promoted him, thus the unrighteous were kept away."

颜渊第十二　Chapter Twelve

孔子说："忠诚地劝告他，恰当地引导他，如果他不听也就罢了，不要自取其辱。"

The Master said, "Advise him sincerely and guide him on the right path. If he repeatedly ignores your advice, then leave him alone. Do not invite humiliation."

【释义】

子贡问交友之道。孔子说："忠诚地劝告他，恰当地引导他，如果他不听也就罢了，不要自取其辱。"

【英译】

Zi Gong asked about friendship. The Master replied, "Advise him sincerely and guide him on the right path. If he repeatedly ignores your advice, then leave him alone. Do not invite humiliation."

12.23
zǐ gòng wèn yǒu　zǐ yuē　zhōng gào ér shàn dǎo zhī　bù kě zé zhǐ
子贡问友。子曰："忠告而善道之，不可则止，
wú zì rǔ yān
毋自辱焉。"

Chapter Twelve 颜渊第十二

曾子说："君子用文章学问来聚会朋友，用朋友来辅助仁德的修养。"

Zeng Zi said, "A man of virtue makes friends through exchange of knowledge, and enhances his ethics through exchange of views with his friends."

【释义】

　　曾子说："君子用文章学问来聚会朋友，用朋友来辅助仁德的修养。"

【英译】

　　Zeng Zi said, "A man of virtue makes friends through exchange of knowledge, and enhances his ethics through exchange of views with his friends."

12.24 zēng zǐ yuē　　jūn zǐ yǐ wén huì yǒu　　yǐ yǒu fǔ rén
曾子曰："君子以文会友，以友辅仁。"

59

zǐ lù dì shí sān
子路第十三
CHAPTER THIRTEEN

Chapter Thirteen 子路第十三

孔子说:"先做表率取信于民,然后再役使人民。"

The Master said, "Take the lead in actions and gain the trust of the people, then engage them in tasks."

【释义】

子路问为政之道。孔子说:"先做表率取信于民,然后再役使人民。"子路请求再多讲一些。孔子说:"不要倦怠。"

【英译】

Zi Lu asked about the way of government. The Master answered, "Take the lead in actions and gain the trust of the people, then engage them in tasks." When Zi Lu asked for more advice, the Master said, "Never be slack."

13.1

zǐ lù wèn zhèng　zǐ yuē　　xiān zhī　láo zhī　　qǐng yì
子路问政。子曰:"先之,劳之。"请益。
yuē　　wú juàn
曰:"无倦。"

子路第十三 Chapter Thirteen

孔子说："给办事人员做表率，宽免别人小的错误，选拔贤良人才。"

The Master said, "Set a good example for your juniors, ignore other people's minor mistakes, and select and promote talented people."

13.2
zhòng gōng wéi jì shì zǎi wèn zhèng zǐ yuē   xiān yǒu sī   shè
仲　弓　为　季　氏　宰，问　政。子曰："先　有　司，赦
xiǎo guò   jǔ xián cái
小　过，举贤才。"
yuē   yān zhī xián cái ér jǔ zhī   yuē   jǔ ěr suǒ zhī
曰："焉　知　贤　才　而举之？"曰："举尔所知。
ěr suǒ bù zhī   rén qí shě zhū
尔　所　不　知，人其舍诸？"

【释义】

仲弓做季氏的家臣，向孔子问为政之道。孔子说："给办事人员做表率，宽免别人小的错误，选拔贤良人才。"

仲弓又说："怎样才能识别贤良人才而把他们选拔出来呢？"孔子说："选拔你所了解的。你所不了解的，别人难道会把他们舍弃吗？"

【英译】

Zhong Gong, steward to the Ji family, asked about the way of government. The Master said, "Set a good example for your juniors, ignore other people's minor mistakes, and select and promote talented people."

Zhong Gong then asked, "How can one distinguish talented people and promote them?" The Master answered, "Promote those whom you recognize. For those whom you fail to recognize, there are surely other people who will recognize and promote them."

Chapter Thirteen 子路第十三

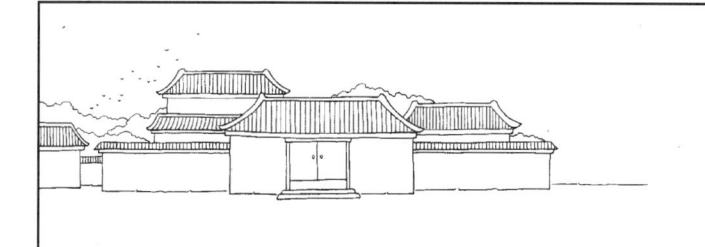

孔子说："混乱的名称不纠正，那么说话就不顺当。"

The Master said, "When names are not proper, what is said will not sound reasonable or convincing."

13.3
子路曰："卫君待子而为政，子将奚先？"
zǐ lù yuē   wèi jūn dài zǐ ér wéi zhèng   zǐ jiāng xī xiān

子曰："必也正名乎！"
zǐ yuē   bì yě zhèng míng hū

子路曰："有是哉，子之迂也！奚其正？"
zǐ lù yuē   yǒu shì zāi   zǐ zhī yū yě   xī qí zhèng

子曰："野哉，由也！君子于其所不知，盖阙如也。"
zǐ yuē   yě zāi   yóu yě   jūn zǐ yú qí suǒ bù zhī   gài quē rú yě

【释义】

子路说："如果卫君等待先生去治理国政，先生将先做什么？"

孔子说："那一定是纠正混乱的名称。"

子路说："先生的迂阔竟有如此严重啊！有什么可纠正的呢？"

孔子说："好粗野啊，子由！君子对他不了解的事情，大概应该避而不谈吧。"

【英译】

Zi Lu asked the Master, "If the ruler of Wei invited you to govern the state for him, what would be your first step?"

The Master replied, "It would be to rectify the names."

Zi Lu said, "You are being so pedantic! What is there to be rectified?"

The Master replied, "How rude of you to say that! A man of virtue does not make assertions on things he does not know."

63

子路第十三 Chapter Thirteen

"名不正，则言不顺；言不顺，则事不成；事不成，则礼乐不兴；礼乐不兴，则刑罚不中，刑罚不中，则民无所措手足。故君子名之必可言也，言之必可行也。君子于其言，无所苟而已矣。"

【释义】

"混乱的名称不纠正，那么说话就不顺当；说话不顺当，那么事情就办不成；事情办不成，那么礼乐就不能兴起；礼乐不能兴起，那么刑罚就不能适中；刑罚不能适中，那么老百姓就会缩手缩脚觉得没有恰当摆放的位置了。因此君子关于正确的名称一定可以顺当地说出来，顺当说出来的事情一定可以行得通。君子对于自己的言辞，力求没有一点儿马虎的地方才算罢了。"

【英译】

"When names are not proper, what is said will not sound reasonable or convincing; when what is said does not sound reasonable or convincing, actions will not result in success; when actions do not result in success, etiquette and music will not flourish; when etiquette and music do not flourish, punishments will not be imposed properly; when punishments are not imposed properly, the common people will be at a loss as to how to behave. Therefore, a man of virtue believes it imperative to have a proper name. Only on this basis can his words sound reasonable and convincing, and can his instructions be carried out properly. A man of virtue is always careful with his words."

Chapter Thirteen   子路第十三

孔子说："居上位的人讲究礼节，老百姓就没有人敢不尊敬。"

The Master said, "If the high-ranking people are willing to observe the etiquette, then the common people will not dare to show disrespect."

【释义】

　　樊迟向孔子请教如何种田。孔子说："这方面我不如有经验的老农民。"又请教如何种菜。孔子说："这方面我不如有经验的老菜农。"

【英译】

　　Fan Chi asked about farming. The Master answered, "I'm not as good as an experienced farmer." Fan Chi then asked about the planting of vegetables. The Master said, "I am not as experienced as a vegetable grower."

13.4　樊迟请学稼。子曰："吾不如老农。"请学为圃。曰："吾不如老圃。"

65

子路第十三　Chapter Thirteen

樊迟出。子曰："小人哉，樊须也！上好礼，则民莫敢不敬；上好义，则民莫敢不服；上好信，则民莫敢不用情。夫如是，则四方之民襁负其子而至矣，焉用稼？"

【释义】

樊迟出去了。孔子说："樊迟真是个小人啊！居上位的人讲求礼节，老百姓就没有人敢不尊敬；居上位的人讲求道义，老百姓就没有人敢不服从；居上位的人讲求诚信，老百姓就没有人敢不实在。若能如此，那么四方的老百姓就会背负着子女来投靠，哪里用得着自己种庄稼呢？"

【英译】

After Fan Chi left, the Master remarked, "Fan Chi is indeed a petty-minded man! If the high-ranking people are willing to observe the etiquette, then the common people will not dare to show disrespect; if the high-ranking people are virtuous, then the common people will not dare to disobey; if the high-ranking people enjoy integrity, then the common people will not dare not to be loyal. If so, then people from all around will come with their young children attached to their back. So what is the use for a high-ranking man to know about farming?"

Chapter Thirteen 子路第十三

孔子说："熟读了《诗经》三百篇，让他处理政务，却办不通；让他出使四方，又不能独立应对。虽然学了很多，又有什么用呢？"

The Master said, "For a man who cannot do a proper job when asked to deal with government affairs, and who cannot conduct a negotiation independently when assigned as an emissary to another country, even if he is able to recite all the three hundred poems in *The Book of Songs*, what is the use of that?"

13.5
zǐ yuē sòng shī sān bǎi shòu zhī yǐ zhèng bù dá shǐ
子曰："诵《诗》三百，授之以政，不达；使
yú sì fāng bù néng zhuān duì suī duō yì xī yǐ wéi
于四方，不能专对；虽多，亦奚以为？"

【释义】

孔子说："熟读了《诗经》三百篇，让他处理政务，却办不通；让他出使四方，又不能独立应对；即使学了很多，又有什么用呢？"

【英译】

The Master said, "For a man who cannot do a proper job when asked to deal with government affairs, and who cannot conduct a negotiation independently when assigned as an emissary to another country, even if he is able to recite all the three hundred poems in *The Book of Songs*, what is the use of that?"

子路第十三　Chapter Thirteen

孔子说:"统治者自身端正了,即使不发布命令,老百姓也会去干。"

The Master said, "If a ruler himself is upstanding, then the people will conduct themselves well even without the ruler giving orders."

13.6
zǐ yuē　　qí shēn zhèng　 bú lìng ér xíng　　qí shēn bú zhèng　suī lìng
子曰:"其身正,不令而行;其身不正,虽令
bù cóng
不从。"

【释义】

孔子说:"统治者自身端正了,即使不发布命令,老百姓也会去干;统治者自身不端正,即使发布命令,老百姓也不会服从。"

【英译】

The Master said, "If a ruler himself is upstanding, then the people will conduct themselves well even without the ruler giving orders; but if the ruler himself is not upstanding, then even if he gives orders, people will not obey."

Chapter Thirteen 子路第十三

孔子说："鲁国、卫国的政治，像兄弟一样相近。"

The Master said, "In terms of politics, the State of Lu and the State of Wei are as close as brothers."

【释义】

孔子说："鲁国、卫国的政治，像兄弟一样相近。"

【英译】

The Master said, "In terms of politics, the State of Lu and the State of Wei are as close as brothers."

13.7

zǐ yuē　　　　lǔ wèi zhī zhèng　xiōng dì yě
子曰："鲁卫之政，兄弟也。"

子路第十三　Chapter Thirteen

In commenting on Prince Jing of the State of Wei, the Master said, "He is good at running his home."

13.8
zǐ wèi wèi gōng zǐ jīng　　shàn jū shì　　shǐ yǒu　yuē　　gǒu hé
子谓卫公子荆："善居室。始有，曰：'苟合
yǐ　　shǎo yǒu　　yuē　gǒu wán yǐ　　　fù yǒu　yuē　　gǒu
矣。'少有，曰：'苟完矣。'富有，曰：'苟
měi yǐ
美矣。'"

【释义】

孔子评论卫国公子荆说："他善于持家过日子。刚有一点儿财产，便说：'实在是足够了。'稍稍增加一些，便说：'实在是太完备了。'富有以后，便说：'实在是太华美了。'"

【英译】

In commenting on Prince Jing of the State of Wei, the Master said, "He is good at running his home. When he had some property, he said, 'This is enough.' When he had a bit more, he said, 'This is substantial enough.' When he became wealthy, he remarked, 'This is indeed magnificent.'"

Chapter Thirteen 子路第十三

孔子说:"人民已经富裕起来了,应当教育人民。"

The Master said, "After the people get rich, the ruler should educate them."

13.9
zǐ shì wèi rǎn yǒu pú zǐ yuē shù yǐ zāi
子适卫,冉有仆。子曰:"庶矣哉!"
rǎn yǒu yuē jì shù yǐ yòu hé jiā yān yuē fù zhī
冉有曰:"既庶矣,又何加焉?"曰:"富之。"
yuē jì fù yǐ yòu hé jiā yān yuē jiào zhī
曰:"既富矣,又何加焉?"曰:"教之。"

【释义】

孔子到卫国,冉有给他驾车。孔子说:"人口好多啊!"

冉有说:"人口已经很多了,再该采取什么措施呢?"孔子说:"使人民富裕起来。"

冉有又说:"已经富裕起来了,又该采取什么措施呢?"孔子说:"教育人民。"

【英译】

The Master was making a trip to the State of Wei, and Ran You was driving the carriage for him. The Master remarked, "What a large population!"

Ran You asked, "What measures should be taken with such a large population?" The Master answered, "Help them become rich."

Ran You then asked, "Suppose they are already rich, what else should be done?" The Master replied, "Educate them."

子路第十三　Chapter Thirteen

孔子说："如果有人用我治理国家，一年就能治理得差不多，三年就能卓有成效。"

The Master said, "If I am asked to govern a state, I'd be able to put it in good shape in a year's time. In three years' time, all my policies will prove fruitful."

【释义】

孔子说："如果有人用我治理国家，一年就能治理得差不多，三年就能卓有成效。"

【英译】

The Master said, "If I am asked to govern a state, I'd be able to put it in good shape in a year's time. In three years' time, all my policies will prove fruitful."

13.10

zǐ yuē　　gǒu yǒu yòng wǒ zhě　　jī yuè ér yǐ kě yě　　sān nián yǒu chéng
子曰："苟有用我者，期月而已可也，三年有成。"

Chapter Thirteen 子路第十三

孔子说："'善人治理国家一百年，也可以克服残暴、消除杀戮了。'这话说得真对呀！"

The Master said, "A state that has been governed by rulers of virtue for a hundred years could get rid of both cruelty and killing. I totally agree with this saying."

【释义】

孔子说："'善人治理国家一百年，也可以克服残暴、消除杀戮了。'这话说得真对呀！"

【英译】

The Master said, "A state that has been governed by rulers of virtue for a hundred years could get rid of both cruelty and killing. I totally agree with this saying."

13.11 zǐ yuē　　　shàn rén wéi bāng bǎi nián　　yì kě yǐ shèng cán qù shā yǐ
子曰："'善人为邦百年，亦可以胜残去杀矣。'
chéng zāi shì yán yě
诚哉是言也！"

子路第十三　Chapter Thirteen

【释义】

孔子说:"如果有称王天下的人出现,也一定要经过三十年才能使仁德普行。"

【英译】

The Master said, "Even for a very competent ruler, it will take thirty years for his humane policies to come to fruition."

孔子说:"如果有称王天下的人出现,也一定要经过三十年才能使仁德普行。"

The Master said, "Even for a very competent ruler, it will take thirty years for his humane policies to come to fruition."

13.12
zǐ yuē　　　rú yǒu wàng zhě　　bì shì ér hòu rén
子曰:"如有王者,必世而后仁。"

Chapter Thirteen 子路第十三

孔子说："如果自身的行为端正了，对于参政治国有什么难的呢？"

The Master said, "If a ruler is upright himself, what difficulty will there be for him to govern a state?"

【释义】

孔子说："如果自身的行为端正了，对于参政治国有什么难的呢？不能端正自身的行为，怎能去端正别人呢？"

【英译】

The Master said, "If a ruler is upright himself, what difficulty will there be for him to govern a state? But if he himself is not upright, then how could he possibly rectify the behavior of other people?"

13.13
zǐ yuē　　gǒu zhèng qí shēn yǐ　　yú cóng zhèng hū　hé yǒu　　bù néng
子曰："苟 正 其 身 矣，于 从 政 乎 何 有？不 能
zhèng qí shēn　　rú zhèng rén hé
正 其 身，如 正 人 何？"

子路第十三 Chapter Thirteen

孔子说："如果有政务，即使不用我了，我也该知道的。"

The Master said, "If they were indeed state affairs, I should have known about them even though I am no longer employed by the state."

13.14
rǎn zǐ tuì cháo　zǐ yuē　　 hé yàn yě　duì yuē　　yǒu
冉子退朝。子曰："何晏也？"对曰："有
zhèng　zǐ yuē　　qí shì yě　 rú yǒu zhèng　suī bù wú yǐ
政。"子曰："其事也。如有政，虽不吾以，
wú qí yù wén zhī
吾其与闻之。"

【释义】

冉有从季氏办公内朝退下。孔子说："为什么这样晚呢？"回答说："有政务。"孔子说："那是事务呀。如果有政务，即使不用我了，我也该知道的。"

【英译】

Ran Zi (Ran You) returned from court headed by the Ji family. The Master asked, "Why so late?" Ran You answered, "There were state affairs to deal with." To that the Master remarked, "Those were just affairs. If they were indeed state affairs, I should have known about them even though I am no longer employed by the state."

Chapter Thirteen 子路第十三

孔子说："一句话可以使国家兴盛，一句话也可以使国家灭亡。"

The Master said, "A single sentence can help a country prosper, and a single sentence may cause a country to be destroyed."

13.15

dìng gōng wèn　　　　yì yán ér kě yǐ xīng bāng　　yǒu zhū
定　公　问："一　言　而　可　以　兴　邦，有　诸？"
kǒng zǐ duì yuē　　　yán bù kě yǐ ruò shì qí jī yě　　rén zhī yán
孔　子　对　曰："言　不　可　以　若　是　其　几　也。人　之　言
yuē　　wéi jūn nán　　wéi chén bú yì　　rú zhī wéi jūn zhī nán yě
曰：'为　君　难，为　臣　不　易。'如　知　为　君　之　难　也，
bù jī hū yì yán ér xīng bāng hū
不　几　乎　一　言　而　兴　邦　乎？"

【释义】

鲁定公问道："一句话就可以使国家兴盛，有这样的话吗？"

孔子回答说："话不可能这样起作用。跟这相近的情况，人们常说：'做君主难，做臣下也不容易。'如果知道做君主的难处是什么，不是接近于一句话就可以使国家兴盛吗？"

【英译】

Duke Ding of the State of Lu asked, "Is there a single sentence that can help a country prosper?"

The Master replied, "Words may not have so much power, but people often say 'It is difficult to be a ruler, nor is it easy to be a subject.'" If a ruler really knows the difficulty in governance, isn't this almost equal to one single sentence helping a country prosper?"

子路第十三 Chapter Thirteen

曰："一言而丧邦，有诸？"
孔子对曰："言不可以若是其几也。人之言曰：'予无乐乎为君，唯其言而莫予违也。'如其善而莫之违也，不亦善乎？如不善而莫之违也，不几乎一言而丧邦乎？"

【释义】

鲁定公又问："一句话就可以使国家灭亡，有这样的话吗？"

孔子回答说："话不可能这样起作用。跟这相近的情况，人们常说：'作为君主，我没有什么快乐的，只是无论我说什么话都没有人违抗。'如果说的话正确而没有人违抗他，不是很好吗？如果说的话不正确而没有人违抗他，不是接近于一句话就会使国家灭亡吗？"

【英译】

Duke Ding then asked, "Is there a single sentence that can cause a country to be destroyed?"

The Master answered, "Words may not have so much power, but people often say 'Nothing makes me happier as a ruler than the fact that whatever I say, no one dares to defy me.' It is fine if no one defies the ruler when his words are reasonable, but if no one dares to defy the ruler when his words are unreasonable, isn't this almost equal to one single sentence causing a country to be destroyed?"

Chapter Thirteen 子路第十三

孔子说:"境内的人使他们欢悦,远方的人使他们来归附。"

The Master said, "The local people are pleased, and people from afar come and join."

【释义】

叶公问怎么治理政事。孔子说:"境内的人使他们欢悦,远方的人使他们来归附。"

【英译】

Lord She, an official, asked about the evidence of good government. The Master answered, "The local people are pleased, and people from afar come and join."

13.16
shè gōng wèn zhèng　　zǐ yuē　　jìn zhě yuè　　yuǎn zhě lái
叶公问政。子曰:"近者说,远者来。"

79

子路第十三 Chapter Thirteen

【释义】

子夏做莒父邑的长官,问为政之道。孔子说:"不要贪图快,不要只见小利。贪图快,就不能达到目的;只见小利,那么大事就不能成功。"

【英译】

Zi Xia became the officer of a county named Jufu, and he asked about ways for good government. The Master answered, "Do not rush, and ignore minor benefits. Rushing often leads to failures, and minor benefits may distract you from achieving major goals."

孔子说:"贪图快,就不能达到目的;只见小利,那么大事就不能成功。"

The Master said, "Rushing often leads to failures, and minor benefits may distract you from achieving major goals."

13.17
zǐ xià wéi jǔ fǔ zǎi　wèn zhèng　zǐ yuē　　wú yù sù　　wú jiàn
子夏为莒父宰,问政。子曰:"无欲速,无见
xiǎo lì　　yù sù zé bù dá　　jiàn xiǎo lì zé dà shì bù chéng
小利。欲速则不达,见小利则大事不成。"

Chapter Thirteen 子路第十三

孔子对叶公说:"我家乡的正直的人和你讲的正直的人不一样:父亲为儿子隐瞒,儿子为父亲隐瞒,正直就体现在这里面。"

The Master said to Lord She, "In my hometown, the upright people behave in a different way: a father would cover up for his son, and a son would cover up for his father. This can be considered as being upright."

13.18
shè gōng yù kǒng zǐ yuē　　wú dǎng yǒu zhí gōng zhě　　qí fù rǎng yáng
叶公语孔子曰:"吾党有直躬者,其父攘羊,
ér zǐ zhèng zhī　　kǒng zǐ yuē　　wú dǎng zhī zhí zhě yì yú shì
而子证之。"孔子曰:"吾党之直者异于是:
fù wèi zǐ yǐn　　zǐ wèi fù yǐn　　zhí zài qí zhōng yǐ
父为子隐,子为父隐,直在其中矣。"

【释义】

叶公告诉孔子说:"我们那里有个行为耿直的人,他的父亲偷了别人的羊,他亲自告发了父亲。"孔子说:"我们那里的正直人与此不同:父亲为儿子隐瞒,儿子为父亲隐瞒,正直也就在里面了。"

【英译】

Lord She told the Master, "In my village there is an upright man. His father had stolen other people's sheep, and he reported his father to the local officials." The Master answered, "In my hometown, the upright people behave in a different way: a father would cover up for his son, and a son would cover up for his father. This can be considered as being upright."

81

子路第十三　Chapter Thirteen

孔子说:"平常在家要恭敬有礼,办事要严肃谨慎,待人要忠心诚意。"

The Master said, "When at home, be courteous and respectful; when at work, be conscientious and prudent; in dealing with people, be sincere and honest."

13.19
fán chí wèn rén　zǐ yuē　　jū chǔ gōng　zhí shì jìng　yǔ rén zhōng
樊迟问仁。子曰:"居处恭,执事敬,与人忠。
suī zhī yí dí　bù kě qì yě
虽之夷狄,不可弃也。"

【释义】

樊迟问什么是仁。孔子说:"平常在家要恭敬有礼,办事要严肃谨慎,待人要忠心诚意。即使到了夷狄地区,也是不可废弃的。"

【英译】

Fan Chi asked about benevolence. The Master replied, "When at home, be courteous and respectful; when at work, be conscientious and prudent; in dealing with people, be sincere and honest. This is a principle that you should follow wherever you are, even when among the (ignorant and backward) *yidi* ethnic groups."

Chapter Thirteen 子路第十三

孔子说:"用羞耻心来约束自己的行为,出使国外,不辱负君主的使命,便可以称得上是士了。"

The Master said, "Those who constrain themselves with a sense of shame and are able to safeguard the dignity of their states and fulfill their mission when sent as envoys to other states can be said as noble."

13.20

zǐ gòng wèn yuē　　　hé rú sī kě wèi zhī shì yǐ　　　　zǐ yuē　　　xíng
子贡问曰:"何如斯可谓之士矣?"子曰:"行
jǐ yǒu chǐ　　shǐ yú sì fāng　　bù rǔ jūn mìng　　kě wèi shì yǐ
己有耻,使于四方,不辱君命,可谓士矣。"
yuē　　gǎn wèn qí cì　　yuē　　zōng zú chēng xiào yān　　xiāng dǎng
曰:"敢问其次。"曰:"宗族称孝焉,乡党
chēng tì yān
称弟焉。"

【释义】

子贡问道:"怎样才可以称得上是士?"孔子说:"用羞耻心来约束自己的行为,出使国外,不辜负君主的使命,便可以称得上是士了。"

子贡说:"请问次一等的。"孔子说:"宗族称赞他孝顺父母,乡里称赞他尊敬兄长。"

【英译】

Zi Gong asked, "What kind of people can be called noble?" The Master replied, "Those who constrain themselves with a sense of shame and are able to safeguard the dignity of their states and fulfill their mission when sent as envoys to other states can be said as noble."

Zi Gong asked further, "What kind of people rank immediately lower than that?" The Master replied, "Those who are praised by members of their own clan as filial and complimented by their neighbors and fellow villagers as friendly and amicable."

子路第十三　Chapter Thirteen

曰："敢问其次。"曰："言必信，行必果，硜硜然小人哉！抑亦可以为次矣。"
曰："今之从政者何如？"子曰："噫！斗筲之人，何足算也！"

【释义】

子贡说："请问再次一等的。"孔子说："说话一定要信实，做事一定要果敢，这是固执而不懂得权变的小人呀！不过也可算是再次一等的士了。"

子贡又说："现在执政的人怎么样？"孔子说："咳！这些心胸狭小的人，哪里能算得上呢？"

【英译】

Zi Gong then asked, "What kind of people rank immediately lower than that?" The Master replied, "Those who always keep their promises and persist in their effort in doing things, though sometimes they may be as shallow and stubborn as petty-minded men."

When Zi Gong asked for the Master's opinion about the people in power, the latter remarked, "Those are narrow-minded people. How can they be called noble?"

Chapter Thirteen 子路第十三

孔子说:"如果不能与按中庸原则行事的人结交的话,那一定要结交狂狷之士!狂者勇于进取,狷者洁身自好。"

The Master said, "If one can not associate with people who conform to the golden mean, then associate with the ambitious and the upright. The former are enterprising and the latter will not do evil things."

【释义】

孔子说:"如果不能与按中庸原则行事的人结交的话,那一定要结交狂狷之士!狂者勇于进取,狷者洁身自好。"

【英译】

The Master said, "If one cannot associate with people who conform to the golden mean, then associate with the ambitious and the upright. The former are enterprising and the latter will not do evil things."

13.21 子曰:"不得中行而与之,必也狂狷乎!狂者进取,狷者有所不为也。"

子路第十三 Chapter Thirteen

《周易》中有这样的话："不坚守德行，有可能受到羞辱。"

In *The Book of Changes*, there is such a line, "Inconstancy in virtue may incur shame."

13.22
子曰："南人有言曰：'人而无恒，不可以作巫医。'善夫！""不恒其德，或承之羞。"子曰："不占而已矣。"

【释义】

孔子说："南方人有句话说：'人如果没有恒心，不可以做巫医。'这话好极了！"

《周易》中有这样的话："不坚守德行，有可能受到羞辱。"孔子说："这是告诉没有恒心坚守德行的人不必去占卦罢了。"

【英译】

The Master said, "People in the south have a saying, 'One who does not have constancy cannot be a doctor.' This is well said!"

In *The Book of Changes*, there is such a line, "Inconstancy in virtue may incur shame." The Master commented, "This is to tell those who are lack of constancy in virtue there is no need to go to astrologers to have their fortune told."

Chapter Thirteen 子路第十三

孔子说："君子讲求和谐而不强求一致，小人讲求一致而不讲和谐。"

The Master said, "A man of virtue advocates harmony with diversity, while a petty-minded man values uniformity instead of harmony."

【释义】

孔子说："君子讲求和谐而不强求一致，小人讲求一致而不讲和谐。"

【英译】

The Master said, "A man of virtue advocates harmony with diversity, while a petty-minded man values uniformity instead of harmony."

13.23
zǐ yuē　　jūn zǐ hé ér bù tóng　xiǎo rén tóng ér bù hé
子曰："君子和而不同，小人同而不和。"

子路第十三　Chapter Thirteen

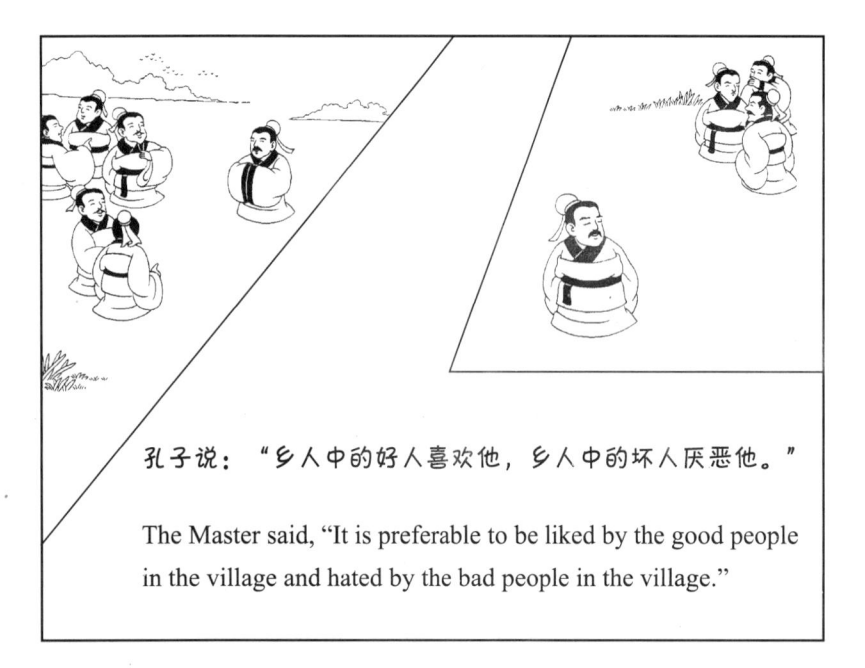

孔子说："乡人中的好人喜欢他，乡人中的坏人厌恶他。"

The Master said, "It is preferable to be liked by the good people in the village and hated by the bad people in the village."

13.24

zǐ gòng wèn yuē　xiāng rén jiē hào zhī　hé rú　zǐ yuē　wèi
子贡问曰："乡人皆好之，何如？"子曰："未
kě yě
可也。"

xiāng rén jiē wù zhī　hé rú　zǐ yuē　wèi kě yě　bù rú
"乡人皆恶之，何如？"子曰："未可也。不如
xiāng rén zhī shàn zhě hào zhī　qí bú shàn zhě wù zhī
乡人之善者好之，其不善者恶之。"

【释义】

　　子贡问道："乡人都喜欢他，怎么样？"孔子说："还不够。"

　　子贡又问："乡人都厌恶他，怎么样？"孔子说："还不够。不如乡人中的好人喜欢他，乡人中的坏人厌恶他。"

【英译】

　　Zi Gong asked, "What do you think of a man who is liked by all his fellow villagers?" The Master answered, "Not good enough."

　　Zi Gong then asked, "What do you think of a man who is hated by all his fellow villagers?" The Master answered, "Not good enough. It is preferable to be liked by the good people in the village and hated by the bad people in the village."

Chapter Thirteen 子路第十三

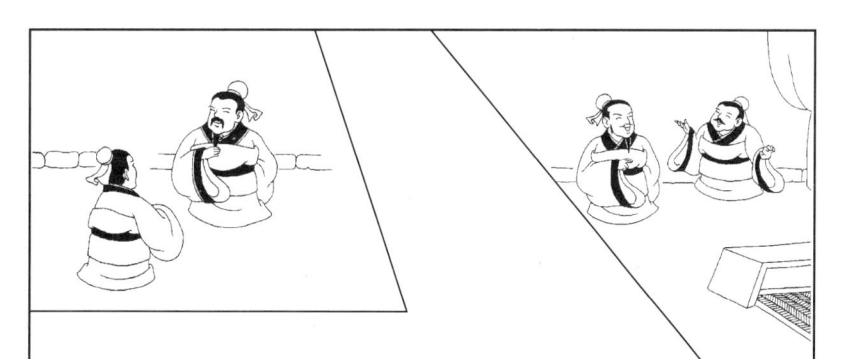

孔子说："君子，容易在他手下做事，却难于讨他喜欢；小人，难于在他手下做事，却容易讨他喜欢。"

The Master said, "A man of virtue is easy to serve, but hard to please. A petty-minded man is hard to serve, but easy to please."

13.25

zǐ yuē jūn zǐ yì shì ér nán yuè yě yuè zhī bù yǐ dào bú
子曰："君子易事而难说也。说之不以道，不
yuè yě jí qí shǐ rén yě qì zhī xiǎo rén nán shì ér yì yuè yě
说也；及其使人也，器之。小人难事而易说也。
yuè zhī suī bù yǐ dào yuè yě jí qí shǐ rén yě qiú bèi yān
说之虽不以道，说也；及其使人也，求备焉。"

【释义】

孔子说："君子，容易在他手下做事，却难于讨他喜欢。不用正当的方法讨他喜欢，他是不会喜欢的；等到他使用别人时，总是量才而用。小人，难于在他手下做事，却容易讨他喜欢。即使不用正当的方法讨他喜欢，他也会喜欢的；等到他使用别人时，总是求全责备。"

【英译】

The Master said, "A man of virtue is easy to serve, but hard to please. If one tried to please him in improper ways, he can not be pleased. When it comes to engaging people for tasks, he always bases his choice on the capability of the candidates. A petty-minded man is hard to serve, but easy to please. He will be pleased even if one tries to please him in improper ways. When it comes to engaging people for tasks, he is always finding faults and demanding perfection."

子路第十三　Chapter Thirteen

【释义】

孔子说:"君子坦然自若,却不骄傲自大;小人骄傲自大,却不坦然自若。"

【英译】

The Master said, "A man of virtue is dignified and graceful, but not rude or self-conceited; In contrast, a petty-minded man is rude and self-conceited, but not dignified or graceful."

孔子说:"君子坦然自若,却不骄傲自大。"

The Master said, "A man of virtue is dignified and graceful, but not rude or self-conceited."

13.26　zǐ yuē　　jūn zǐ tài ér bù jiāo　xiǎo rén jiāo ér bú tài
子曰:"君子泰而不骄,小人骄而不泰。"

Chapter Thirteen   子路第十三

孔子说:"刚强、果敢、朴实、谨言,这四种品质都近于仁。"

The Master said, "Those who are resolute, courageous, natural and sincere, and cautious in words are close to virtue."

【释义】

孔子说:"刚强、果敢、朴实、谨言,这四种品质都近于仁。"

【英译】

The Master said, "Those who are resolute, courageous, natural and sincere, and cautious in words are close to virtue."

13.27
zǐ yuē　　gāng　yì　mù　nè　　jìn rén
子曰:"刚、毅、木、讷,近仁。"

子路第十三 Chapter Thirteen

孔子说："互相勉励督促，和睦相处，便可以称为士了。"

The Master said, "Those who caution each other against making mistakes and urge each other on and at the same time get along harmoniously can be called scholars."

13.28
zǐ lù wèn yuē　　　hé rú sī kě wèi zhī shì yǐ　　zǐ yuē　　qiè
子路问曰："何如斯可谓之士矣？"子曰："切
qiè sī sī　yí yí rú yě　kě wèi shì yǐ　péng yǒu qiè qiè sī sī
切偲偲、怡怡如也，可谓士矣。朋友切切偲偲，
xiōng dì yí yí
兄弟怡怡。"

【释义】

子路问道："怎样才可以叫做士？"孔子说："互相勉励督促，和睦相处，便可以称为士了。朋友之间互相勉励督促，兄弟之间和睦相处。"

【英译】

Zi Lu asked, "What kind of people can be regarded as scholars?" The Master answered, "Those who caution each other against making mistakes and urge each other on and at the same time get along harmoniously can be called scholars. It is desirable for friends to encourage each other and caution each other against blunders. It is equally desirable for brothers to be friendly with each other."

Chapter Thirteen 子路第十三

孔子说："善人教育人民达七年之久，也就可以让他们参军作战了。"

The Master said, "After having been trained by a good man for seven years, the common people can be sent to the battlefields to fight."

【释义】

孔子说："善人教育人民达七年之久，也就可以让他们参军作战了。"

【英译】

The Master said, "After having been trained by a good man for seven years, the common people can be sent to the battlefields to fight."

13.29 zǐ yuē　　shàn rén jiāo mín qī nián　yì kě yǐ jí róng yǐ
子曰："善人教民七年，亦可以即戎矣。"

子路第十三　Chapter Thirteen

【释义】

孔子说:"用未经教育训练的人民作战,这等于说抛弃他们。"

【英译】

The Master said, "To send the people to the battlefields without giving them proper training is tantamount to discarding them."

> 孔子说:"用未经教育训练的人民作战,这等于说抛弃他们。"
>
> The Master said, "To send the people to the battlefields without giving them proper training is tantamount to discarding them."

13.30
zǐ yuē　　　yǐ bú jiào mín zhàn　shì wèi qì zhī
子曰:"以不教民战,是谓弃之。"

xiàn wèn dì shí sì
宪问第十四
CHAPTER FOURTEEN

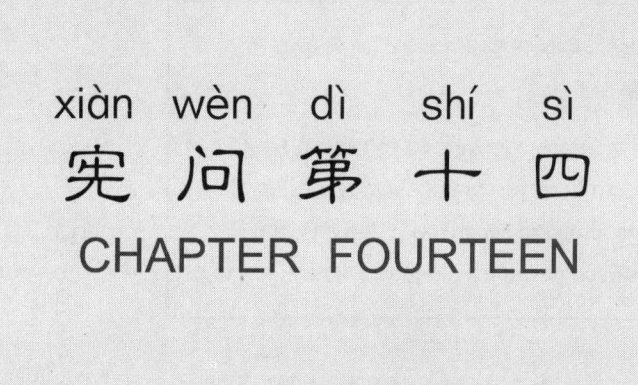

宪问第十四 Chapter Fourteen

孔子说:"国家政治清明,可以做官得俸禄;如果国家政治昏暗,做官得俸禄就是耻辱。"

The Master said, "When the state is governed in accord with the Way, it is fine to hold an official position and enjoy a salary; but when the state is not governed in accord with the Way, then it is shameful to hold an official position and enjoy a salary."

14.1
xiàn wèn chǐ　　zǐ yuē　　　bāng yǒu dào　　gǔ　　bāng wú dào　　gǔ
宪问耻。子曰:"邦有道,谷;邦无道,谷,
chǐ yě
耻也。"

　　kè　fá　yuàn　yù bù xíng yān　　kě yǐ wéi rén yǐ
"克、伐、怨、欲不行焉,可以为仁矣?"
zǐ yuē　　kě yǐ wéi nán yǐ　　rén　zé wú bù zhī yě
子曰:"可以为难矣。仁,则吾不知也。"

【释义】
　　原宪问什么是羞耻。孔子说:"国家政治清明,可以做官得俸禄;如果国家政治昏暗,做官得俸禄就是耻辱。"
　　原宪又问:"一个人没有好胜、自夸、怨恨、贪欲,可以称得上仁了吗?"孔子说:"可以说是难能可贵的了。能否算得上仁,我就不知道了。"

【英译】
　　Yuan Xian asked about shame. The Master answered, "When the state is governed in accord with the Way, it is fine to hold an official position and enjoy a salary; but when the state is not governed in accord with the Way, then it is shameful to hold an official position and enjoy a salary."
　　Yuan Xian then asked, "If a man has shown none of the following: weaknesses, eagerness to outshine others, singing one's own praises, resentment and avarice, can he be called virtuous?" The Master answered, "He can be said as commendable, but whether he can be termed virtuous, I don't know."

Chapter Fourteen 宪问第十四

孔子说:"士如果怀恋乡居之安,就不足以称为士了。"

The Master said, "A man who values material comfort can not be called noble."

【释义】

孔子说:"士如果怀恋乡居之安,就不足以称为士了。"

【英译】

The Master said, "A man who values material comfort can not be called noble."

14.2 zǐ yuē　　shì ér huái jū　bù zú yǐ wéi shì yǐ
子曰:"士而怀居,不足以为士矣。"

宪问第十四　Chapter Fourteen

【释义】

孔子说："国家治道清明，要正直地说话，正直地做人；国家治道昏乱，要正直地做人，说话却要谨慎。"

【英译】

The Master said, "When the state is governed in accord with the Way, one should be upright in both words and deeds; but if the state is not governed in accord with the Way, one should be upright in deeds, but cautious in words."

14.3　子曰："邦有道，危言危行；邦无道，危行言孙。"

Chapter Fourteen   宪问第十四

孔子说："有德行之人一定有善言，有善言之人不一定有德行。"

The Master said, "A man of virtue naturally has kind words, but one who has kind words is not necessarily a man of virtue."

14.4
zǐ yuē　　yǒu dé zhě bì yǒu yán　　yǒu yán zhě bú bì yǒu dé　　rén
子曰："有德者必有言，有言者不必有德。仁
zhě bì yǒu yǒng　　yǒng zhě bú bì yǒu rén
者必有勇，勇者不必有仁。"

【释义】

孔子说："有德行之人一定有善言，有善言之人不一定有德行。有仁德的人一定勇敢，勇敢的人不一定有仁德。"

【英译】

The Master said, "A man of virtue naturally has kind words, but one who has kind words is not necessarily a man of virtue. A man of virtue is sure to be courageous, but a courageous man is not necessarily a man of virtue."

宪问第十四　Chapter Fourteen

【释义】

南宫适向孔子问道："后羿善于射箭，奡力大翻舟，结果都不得好死。大禹和后稷亲自参加农事，却都得到天下。"孔子不回答。

南宫适出去以后，孔子说："这个人真是君子啊！这个人真崇尚道德啊！"

【英译】

Nangong Kuo said to the Master, "Yi was good at archery, and Ao was strong enough to overthrow a boat, yet neither of them died a natural death. In contrast, both Yu and Ji manually toiled at farmland, and yet they both won the empire." The Master did not make any comments.

After Nangong Kuo left, the Master remarked, "This is truly a man of virtue! He truly upholds virtue!"

14.5
nán gōng kuò wèn yú kǒng zǐ yuē　　yì shàn shè　ào dàng zhōu　jù bù
南宫适问于孔子曰："羿善射，奡荡舟，俱不
dé qí sǐ rán　yǔ jì gōng jià　ér yǒu tiān xià　fū zǐ bù dá
得其死然。禹稷躬稼，而有天下。"夫子不答。
nán gōng kuò chū　zǐ yuē　jūn zǐ zāi ruò rén　shàng dé zāi ruò rén
南宫适出。子曰："君子哉若人！尚德哉若人！"

Chapter Fourteen 宪问第十四

孔子说:"身为君子却不具备仁德的人是有的,但没有身为小人却具备仁德的人。"

The Master said, "There are cases where a gentleman is not virtuous, but there are never cases where a petty-minded man is virtuous."

【释义】

孔子说:"身为君子却不具备仁德的人是有的,但没有身为小人却具备仁德的人。"

【英译】

The Master said, "There are cases where a gentleman is not virtuous, but there are never cases where a petty-minded man is virtuous."

14.6

zǐ yuē jūn zǐ ér bù rén zhě yǒu yǐ fú wèi yǒu xiǎo rén ér rén zhě yě
子曰:"君子而不仁者有矣夫,未有小人而仁者也。"

宪问第十四　Chapter Fourteen

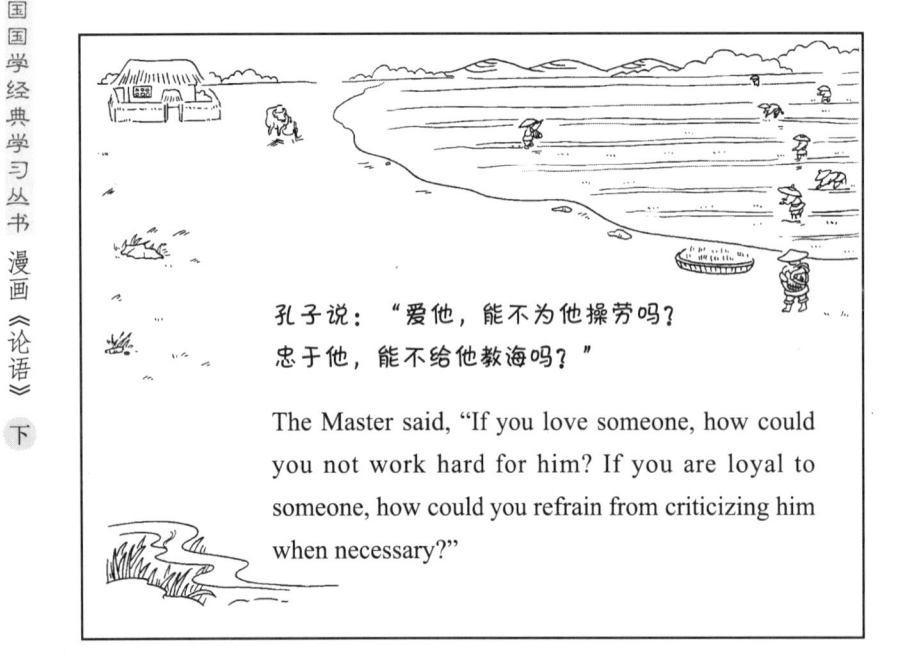

孔子说:"爱他,能不为他操劳吗?
忠于他,能不给他教诲吗?"

The Master said, "If you love someone, how could you not work hard for him? If you are loyal to someone, how could you refrain from criticizing him when necessary?"

【释义】

孔子说:"爱他,能不为他操劳吗?忠于他,能不给他教诲吗?"

【英译】

The Master said, "If you love someone, how could you not work hard for him? If you are loyal to someone, how could you refrain from criticizing him when necessary?"

14.7
zǐ yuē　　ài zhī　　néng wù láo hū　　zhōng yān　　néng wù huì hū
子曰:"爱之,能勿劳乎?忠焉,能勿诲乎?"

Chapter Fourteen 宪问第十四

孔子说:"郑国拟定外交辞令,裨谌先起草稿,世叔加以研讨议论,外交官子羽加以修饰,东里子产加以润色。"

The Master said, "In the State of Zheng, when a diplomatic document was to be issued, Pi Chen wrote the first draft, then Shi Shu studied it and gave constructive suggestions, after that Zi Yu the diplomat revised it, and finally Zi Chan did the polishing."

【释义】

孔子说:"郑国拟定外交辞令,裨谌先起草稿,世叔加以研讨议论,外交官子羽加以修饰,东里子产加以润色。"

【英译】

The Master said, "In the State of Zheng, when a diplomatic document was to be issued, Pi Chen wrote the first draft, then Shi Shu studied it and gave constructive suggestions, after that Zi Yu the diplomat revised it, and finally Zi Chan did the polishing."

14.8 zǐ yuē wéi mìng pí chén cǎo chuàng zhī shì shū tǎo lùn zhī xíng
子曰:"为命,裨谌草创之,世叔讨论之,行
rén zǐ yǔ xiū shì zhī dōng lǐ zǐ chǎn rùn sè zhī
人子羽修饰之,东里子产润色之。"

宪问第十四　Chapter Fourteen

有人问子产是个怎样的人。孔子说："是个宽厚仁慈的人。"

Someone asked about Zi Chan. The Master said, "Zi Chan is kind and generous."

14.9
huò wèn zǐ chǎn　zǐ yuē　　huì rén yě
或问子产。子曰："惠人也。"
wèn zǐ xī　yuē　　bǐ zāi　bǐ zāi
问子西。曰："彼哉！彼哉！"
wèn guǎn zhòng　yuē　　rén yě　duó bó shì pián yì sān bǎi　fàn
问管仲。曰："人也。夺伯氏骈邑三百，饭
shū shí　mò chǐ wú yuàn yán
疏食，没齿无怨言。"

【释义】

有人问子产是个怎样的人。孔子说："是个宽厚仁慈的人。"

又问子西是个怎样的人。孔子说："他呀！他呀！"

又问管仲是个怎样的人。孔子说："是个人才。他剥夺伯氏骈邑三百户的土地，让伯氏只能吃粗饭，然而伯氏直到老死也都没有怨言。"

【英译】

Someone asked about Zi Chan. The Master said, "He is kind and generous."

When asked about Zi Xi, the Master sighed, "Oh, that man! About him!"

When asked about Guan Zhong, the Master said, "He is a real talent. He had managed to take the land of three hundred households from the Bo family in the County of Pian. As a result, the latter had to live on coarse food for the rest of his life, yet he never uttered any complaint."

Chapter Fourteen 宪问第十四

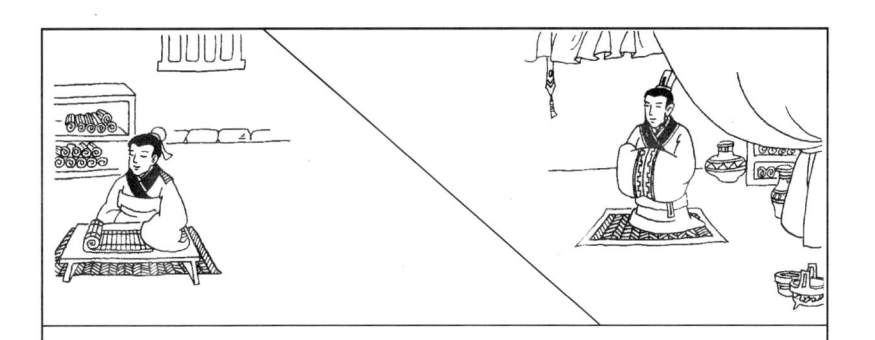

孔子说:"贫穷却没有怨恨,难以做到;富有却没有骄气,容易做到。"

The Master said, "It is difficult for people suffering poverty to refrain from resentment, but it is easy for wealthy people to refrain from being arrogant."

【释义】

孔子说:"贫穷却没有怨恨,难以做到;富有却没有骄气,容易做到。"

【英译】

The Master said, "It is difficult for people suffering poverty to refrain from resentment, but it is easy for wealthy people to refrain from being arrogant."

14.10

zǐ yuē　　pín ér wú yuàn nán　　fù ér wú jiāo yì
子曰:"贫而无怨难,富而无骄易。"

宪问第十四　Chapter Fourteen

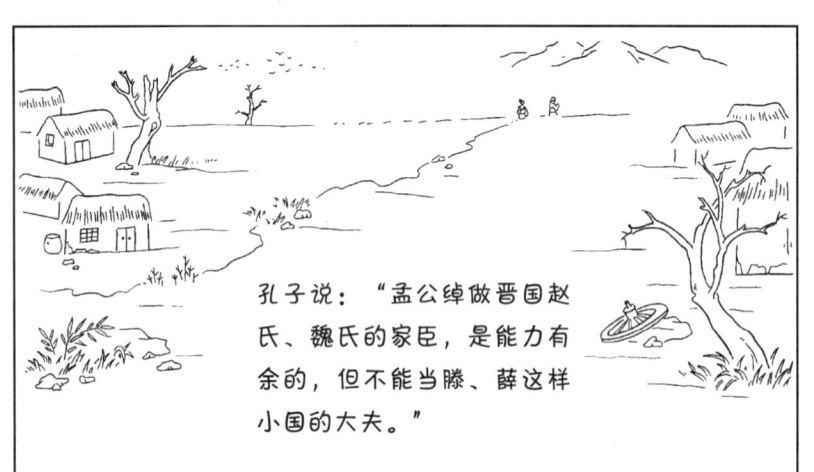

> 孔子说："孟公绰做晋国赵氏、魏氏的家臣，是能力有余的，但不能当滕、薛这样小国的大夫。"

> The Master said, "Meng Gongchuo is more than qualified to be a steward for the Zhao or Wei families in the State of Jin, but he is not qualified to be a minister, not even for such small states as Teng and Xue."

【释义】

孔子说："孟公绰做晋国赵氏、魏氏的家臣，是能力有余的，但不能当滕、薛这样小国的大夫。"

【英译】

The Master said, "Meng Gongchuo is more than qualified to be a steward for the Zhao or Wei families in the State of Jin, but he is not qualified to be a minister, not even for such small states as Teng and Xue."

14.11
zǐ yuē　mèng gōng chuò wéi zhào　wèi lǎo zé yōu　bù kě yǐ wéi
子曰："孟公绰为赵、魏老则优，不可以为
téng　xuē dà fū
滕、薛大夫。"

Chapter Fourteen 宪问第十四

孔子说:"见到利益能想到是否合乎义,见到危难肯于献身,久处困顿境遇而不忘平生所立誓言,也可以称做完美的人了。"

The Master said, "If a man remains righteous in the face of gains, is willing to sacrifice his life in the face of danger, sticks to his promises even after having been in a prolonged difficult situation, then he can be called perfect."

14.12

zǐ lù wèn chéng rén　　zǐ yuē　　　　ruò zāng wǔ zhòng zhī zhì　 gōng chuò zhī
子 路 问 成 人。子 曰:"若 臧 武 仲 之 知,公 绰 之
bú yù　　biàn zhuāng zǐ zhī yǒng　 rǎn qiú zhī yì　　wén zhī yǐ lǐ yuè
不 欲, 卞 庄 子 之 勇, 冉 求 之 艺, 文 之 以 礼 乐,
yì kě yǐ wéi chéng rén yǐ　　　yuē　　jīn zhī chéng rén zhě hé bì rán
亦 可 以 为 成 人 矣。" 曰:"今 之 成 人 者 何 必 然?
jiàn lì sī yì　　jiàn wēi shòu mìng　 jiǔ yāo bú wàng píng shēng zhī yán　 yì
见 利 思 义, 见 危 授 命, 久 要 不 忘 平 生 之 言, 亦
kě yǐ wéi chéng rén yǐ
可 以 为 成 人 矣。"

【释义】

子路问怎样才算是完人。孔子说:"像臧武仲那样的睿智,孟公绰那样的不贪心,卞庄子那样的勇敢,冉求那样的多才多艺,再用礼乐加以修饰,也可以称做完人了。"又说:"现今的完人何必一定如此?见到利益能想到是否合乎义,见到危难肯于献身,久处困顿境遇而不忘平生所立誓言,也可以称做完美的人了。"

【英译】

Zi Lu asked about qualities of a perfect man. The Master answered, "A man can be called perfect if he is as wise as Zang Wuzhong, as free from desires as Meng Gongchuo, as courageous as Bian Zhuangzi, as versatile as Ran Qiu, and is refined by etiquette and music." He then added, "Today's people may not be able to achieve all these, but if a man remains righteous in the face of gains, is willing to sacrifice his life in the face of danger, sticks to his promises even after having been in a prolonged difficult situation, then he can be called perfect."

宪问第十四　Chapter Fourteen

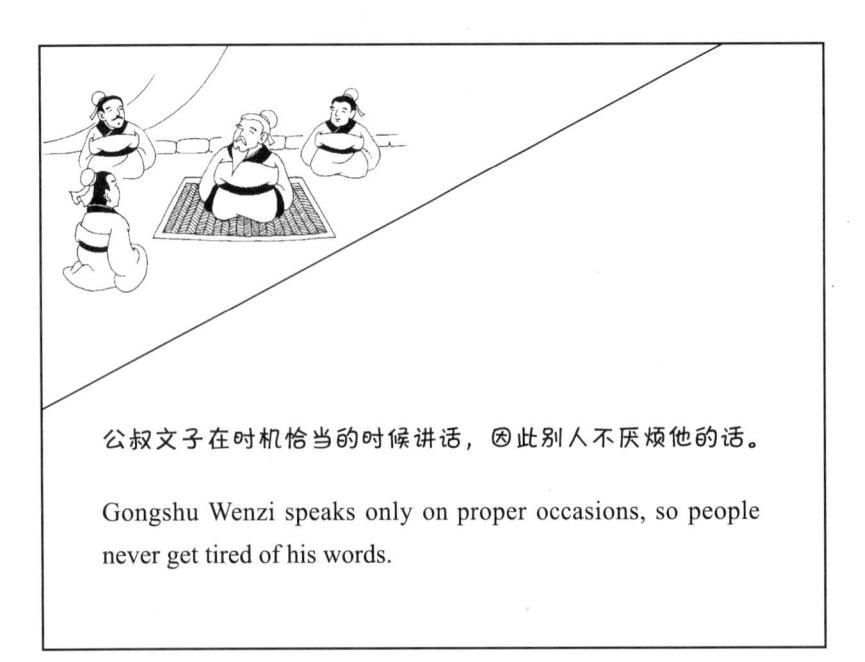

公叔文子在时机恰当的时候讲话，因此别人不厌烦他的话。

Gongshu Wenzi speaks only on proper occasions, so people never get tired of his words.

14.13 子问公叔文子于公明贾曰："信乎？夫子不言、不笑、不取乎？"
公明贾对曰："以告者过也。夫子时然后言，人不厌其言；乐然后笑，人不厌其笑；义然后取，人不厌其取。"子曰："其然，岂其然乎？"

【释义】

孔子向公明贾询问公叔文子，说："当真吗？这位先生不讲话、不笑、不索取吗？"

公明贾说："这是传话人造成的过错。这位先生在时机恰当的时候讲话，因此别人不厌烦他的话；高兴时才笑，因此别人不厌烦他的笑；合乎义然后索取，因此别人不厌烦他的索取。"孔子说："原来是这样，难道真是这样吗？"

【英译】

The Master asked Gongming Gu about Gongshu Wenzi, "Is it true that he never speaks, laughs or takes money or things from others?"

Gongming Gu answered, "Whoever said this about him is wrong. This master speaks only on proper occasions, so people never get tired of his words; he laughs only when he is truly happy, so people never get tired of his laughter; he takes money or things from other people only when he deserves them, so people never get tired of him." The Master said, "Is it so? Is it really so?"

Chapter Fourteen 宪问第十四

孔子说:"臧武仲凭借防邑请求鲁君立他的后代为卿大夫,虽然有人说他不是要挟国君,我可不相信。"

The Master said, "Zang Wuzhong stayed in his fief Fang and pressurized the ruler of the Lu State into appointing one of his blood relatives of a later generation as Minister. Although people say the ruler was not pressurized, I don't think so."

14.14
zǐ yuē　　zāng wǔ zhòng yǐ fáng qiú wéi hòu yú lǔ　　suī yuē bù yāo jūn
子曰:"臧武仲以防求为后于鲁,虽曰不要君,
wú bú xìn yě
吾不信也。"

【释义】

孔子说:"臧武仲凭借防邑请求鲁君立他的后代为卿大夫,虽然有人说他不是要挟国君,我可不相信。"

【英译】

The Master said, "Zang Wuzhong stayed in his fief Fang and pressurized the ruler of the Lu State into appointing one of his blood relatives of a later generation as Minister. Although people say the ruler was not pressurized, I don't think so."

109

宪问第十四　Chapter Fourteen

孔子说："晋文公欺诈而不正直，齐桓公正直而不欺诈。"

The Master said, "Duke Wen of the Jin State is dishonest and crooked, while Duke Huan of the Qi State is honest and upright."

【释义】

孔子说："晋文公欺诈而不正直，齐桓公正直而不欺诈。"

【英译】

The Master commented, "Duke Wen of the Jin State is dishonest and crooked, while Duke Huan of the Qi State is honest and upright."

14.15

zǐ yuē　jìn wén gōng jué ér bú zhèng　qí huán gōng zhèng ér bù jué
子曰："晋文公谲而不正，齐桓公正而不谲。"

Chapter Fourteen 宪问第十四

孔子说:"齐桓公多次会盟诸侯,不动用兵车武力,都是管仲的功劳。这就是他的仁!"

The Master said, "For several times Duke Huan managed to form alliances with other states without using any military force. The credit should be given to Guan Zhong. This is evidence of his virtue."

14.16

zǐ lù yuē huán gōng shā gōng zǐ jiū shào hū sǐ zhī guǎn zhòng bù
子路曰:"桓公杀公子纠,召忽死之,管仲不
sǐ yuē wèi rén hū zǐ yuē huán zhòng jiǔ hé zhū
死。"曰:"未仁乎?"子曰:"桓公九合诸
hóu bù yǐ bīng chē guǎn zhòng zhī lì yě rú qí rén rú qí rén
侯,不以兵车,管仲之力也。如其仁!如其仁!"

【释义】

子路说:"齐桓公杀了公子纠,召忽为主子自杀而死,管仲却不死。"接着又说:"管仲还未达到仁吧?"孔子说:"齐桓公多次会盟诸侯,不动用兵车武力,都是管仲的功劳。这就是他的仁!这就是他的仁!"

【英译】

Zi Lu remarked, "Duke Huan of the Qi State killed Prince Jiu. While Shao Hu committed suicide to show his loyalty, Guan Zhong didn't." Then he asked, "Guang Zhong can't be said as virtuous, can he?" The Master answered, "For several times Duke Huan managed to form alliances with other states without using any military force. The credit should be given to Guan Zhong. This is evidence of his virtue; this is evidence of his virtue."

宪问第十四　Chapter Fourteen

孔子说："管仲辅佐桓公，称霸诸侯，匡正了天下，百姓直到今天还受他的好处。"

The Master said, "Guan Zhong, as the Prime Minister of Duke Huan, helped the latter in conquering the dukes of other states and in maintaining a good social order. Even today people are still benefiting from what Guan Zhong did."

14.17

zǐ gòng yuē　guǎn zhòng fēi rén zhě yú　huán gōng shā gōng zǐ jiū bù
子贡曰："管仲非仁者与？桓公杀公子纠，不
néng sǐ　yòu xiàng zhī　zǐ yuē　guǎn zhòng xiàng huán gōng　bà
能死，又相之。"子曰："管仲相桓公，霸
zhū hóu　yì kuāng tiān xià　mín dào yú jīn shòu qí cì　wēi guǎn zhòng
诸侯，一匡天下，民到于今受其赐。微管仲，
wú qí pī fà zuǒ rèn yǐ　qǐ ruò pǐ fū pǐ fù zhī wéi liàng yě　zì
吾其披发左衽矣！岂若匹夫匹妇之为谅也，自
jīng yú gōu dú ér mò zhī zhī yě
经于沟渎而莫之知也？"

【释义】

子贡说："管仲不是仁人吧？齐桓公杀了公子纠，他不能为公子纠殉死，还去做桓公的宰相。"孔子说："管仲辅佐桓公，称霸诸侯，匡正了天下，百姓直到今天还受他的好处。如果没有管仲，我们恐怕也要披散头发，衣襟向左开了。哪里能像普通男女那样讲小节小信，自杀死在山沟里，而谁也不知道呢？"

【英译】

Zi Gong asked, "Guan Zhong cannot be counted as a man of virtue, can he? Duke Huan of the Qi State killed Prince Jiu, yet, as Duke Jiu's Minister, Guan Zhong did not commit suicide to show his loyalty, instead, he served Duke Huan as the Prime Minister." The Master said, "Guan Zhong, as the Prime Minister of Duke Huan, helped the latter in conquering the dukes of other states and in maintaining a good social order. Even today people are still benefiting from what Guan Zhong did. If it were not for Guang Zhong, we might still be living a barbarian life. It is unreasonable for you to expect Guan Zhong to focus on trivial things and behave like an ordinary man or woman."

Chapter Fourteen 宪问第十四

Note: Guan Zhong was originally serving Prince Jiu, the brother of Duke Huan of the Qi State. In their fight for power, Duke Huan of the Qi State killed his brother. In defending his former master, Guan Zhong shot an arrow at Duke Huan, and the latter was nearly killed. However, Duke Huan of the Qi State did not choose to kill Guan Zhong; instead, he made him his Prime Minister. Confucius gave the above comments when one of his disciples questioned the virtues of Guan Zhong because he did not show his loyalty to his former master by committing suicide after his master's death.

宪问第十四　Chapter Fourteen

孔子说："公叔文子可以称为'文'了。"

The Master said, "Gongshu Wenzi indeed deserves the posthumous title *wen* (the cultured)."

【释义】

公叔文子的家臣大夫僎与公叔文子一起升到卫国公室做官。孔子听到后，说："公叔文子可以称为'文'了。"

【英译】

Gongshu Wenzi's and his steward were both promoted as ministers of the Lu State. Upon hearing this, the Master said, "Gongshu Wenzi indeed deserves the posthumous title *wen* (the cultured)."

14.18 gōng shū wén zǐ zhī chén dà fū zhuàn yǔ wén zǐ tóng shēng zhū gōng　zǐ wén
公叔文子之臣大夫僎与文子同升诸公。子闻
zhī　yuē　　kě yǐ wéi wén yǐ
之，曰："可以为'文'矣。"

Chapter Fourteen 宪问第十四

孔子说:"卫灵公他有仲叔圉主管外交,祝鮀主管祭祀,王孙贾主管军队。既然如此,那又怎么会败亡呢?"

The Master said, "Duke Ling of the Wei State has Zhongshu Yu in charge of foreign affairs, Zhu Tuo of sacrifice and Wangsun Gu of military affairs. That's why he can still rule the state."

14.19
zǐ yán wèi líng gōng zhī wú dào yě, kāng zǐ yuē: "fú rú shì, xī
子言卫灵公之无道也,康子曰:"夫如是,奚
ér bú sàng? kǒng zǐ yuē zhòng shū yǔ zhì bīn kè zhù tuó zhì
而不丧?"孔子曰:"仲叔圉治宾客,祝鮀治
zōng miào wáng sūn gǔ zhì jūn lǚ fú rú shì xī qí sàng
宗庙,王孙贾治军旅。夫如是,奚其丧?"

【释义】

孔子谈论卫灵公的昏乱无道,季康子说:"既然如此,为什么不败亡呢?"孔子说:"他有仲叔圉主管外交,祝鮀主管祭祀,王孙贾主管军队。既然如此,那又怎么会败亡呢?"

【英译】

The Master was talking about the unprincipled reign of Duke Ling of the Wei State. Ji Kangzi asked, "Such being the case, why could he still rule the state?" The Master answered, "Because he has Zhongshu Yu in charge of foreign affairs, Zhu Tuo of sacrifice and Wangsun Gu of military affairs. This is why he can still rule the state."

宪问第十四　Chapter Fourteen

【释义】

孔子说："一个人大言不惭，那他实践起来一定很困难。"

【英译】

The Master said, "If a man talks big, then it will be difficult for him to put his words into action."

孔子说："一个人大言不惭，那他实践起来一定很困难。"

The Master said, "If a man talks big, then it will be difficult for him to put his words into action."

14.20
zǐ yuē　　　qí yán zhī bú zuò　　zé wéi zhī yě nán
子曰："其言之不怍，则为之也难。"

Chapter Fourteen 宪问第十四

齐国大臣陈成子杀了齐简公。孔子说:"因为我忝居大夫之列,不敢不报告这样重大的事啊。"

Chen Chengzi, a minister of the Qi State murdered his sovereign Duke Jian. The Master remarked, "It was because I was once a minister that I did not dare not to report such a major incident."

14.21

chén chéng zǐ shì jiǎn gōng　kǒng zǐ mù yù ér cháo　gào yú āi gōng yuē
陈 成 子 弑 简 公。孔 子 沐 浴 而 朝,告 于 哀 公 曰:

chén héng shì qí jūn　qǐng tǎo zhī　gōng yuē　gào fú sān zǐ
"陈 恒 弑 其 君,请 讨 之。"公 曰:"告 夫 三 子。"

kǒng zǐ yuē　yǐ wú cóng dà fū zhī hòu　bù gǎn bú gào yě　jūn
孔 子 曰:"以 吾 从 大 夫 之 后,不 敢 不 告 也。君

yuē　gào fú sān zǐ　zhě
曰 '告 夫 三 子' 者。"

【释义】

齐国大臣陈成子杀了齐简公。孔子斋戒沐浴以后上朝报告鲁哀公说:"陈恒杀了他的君主,请出兵讨伐他。"哀公说:"那就报告孟孙、叔孙、季孙三人吧!"

孔子退下后说:"因为我忝居大夫之列之后,不敢不报告这样重大的事啊。君主竟说出'报告三子'的话!"

【英译】

Chen Chengzi, a minister of the Qi State murdered his sovereign Duke Jian. After a fast and a bath, Confucius went to the court of Lu to report the incident to Duke Ai, "Chen Heng has murdered his sovereign. Please send an expeditionary force to punish him." Duke Ai answered, "Report it to the Three Lords (Mengsun, Shusun and Jisun)."

After having left the court, the Master remarked, "It was because I was once a minister that I did not dare not to report such a major incident. Yet I never expected the sovereign would ask me to 'Report it to the Three Lords.'"

宪问第十四 Chapter Fourteen

之三子告，不可。孔子曰："以吾从大夫之后，不敢不告也。"

【释义】

于是到了孟孙、叔孙、季孙三人那里报告，结果是三人不同意出兵。孔子说："因为我忝居大夫行列之后，不敢不报告这样重大的事啊！"

【英译】

He then went to report to the Three Lords, but they refused to take any action. The Master sighed, "It was only because I was once a minister that I did not dare not to report such a major incident!"

Chapter Fourteen 宪问第十四

孔子说:"不要欺骗君主,而应该当面说实话来规劝他。"

The Master said, "Do not be dishonest to the ruler for the sake of compliance, instead, be courageous and tell him the truth even if he may feel offended."

【释义】

子路问怎样侍奉君主。孔子说:"不要欺骗他,而应该当面说实话来规劝他。"

【英译】

Zi Lu asked for advice for serving a ruler. The Master said, "Do not be dishonest for the sake of compliance, instead, be courageous and tell him the truth even if he may feel offended."

14.22 zǐ lù wèn shì jūn　zǐ yuē　　wù qī yě　　ér fàn zhī
子路问事君。子曰:"勿欺也,而犯之。"

119

宪问第十四　Chapter Fourteen

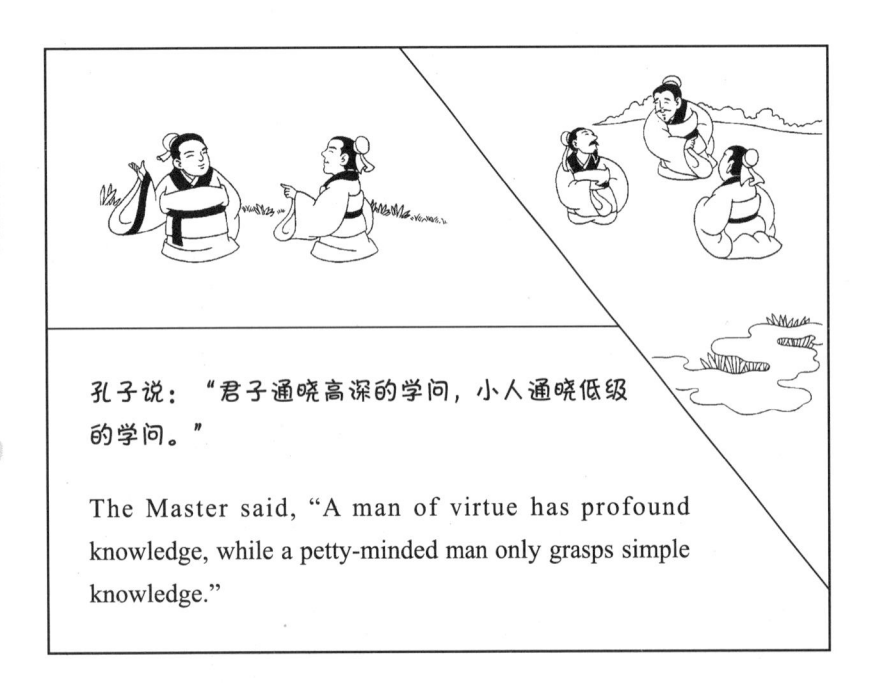

【释义】

孔子说:"君子通晓高深的学问,小人通晓低级的学问。"

【英译】

The Master said, "A man of virtue has profound knowledge, while a petty-minded man only grasps simple knowledge."

孔子说:"君子通晓高深的学问,小人通晓低级的学问。"

The Master said, "A man of virtue has profound knowledge, while a petty-minded man only grasps simple knowledge."

14.23
zǐ yuē　　jūn zǐ shàng dá　　xiǎo rén xià dá
子曰:"君子上达,小人下达。"

Chapter Fourteen 宪问第十四

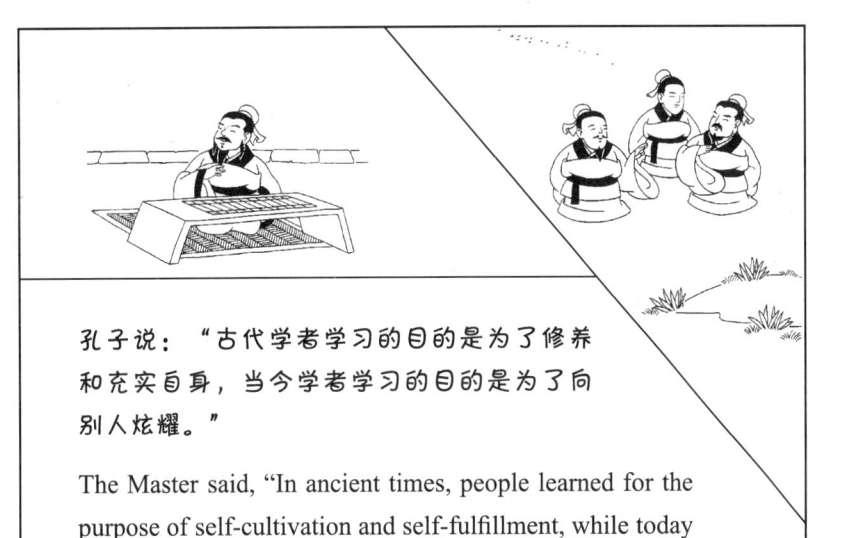

孔子说:"古代学者学习的目的是为了修养和充实自身,当今学者学习的目的是为了向别人炫耀。"

The Master said, "In ancient times, people learned for the purpose of self-cultivation and self-fulfillment, while today people learn for the purpose of impressing other people."

【释义】

孔子说:"古代学者学习的目的是为了修养和充实自身,当今学者学习的目的是为了向别人炫耀。"

【英译】

The Master said, "In ancient times, people learned for the purpose of self-cultivation and self-fulfillment, while today people learn for the purpose of impressing other people."

14.24

zǐ yuē　　gǔ zhī xué zhě wèi jǐ　　jīn zhī xué zhě wèi rén
子曰:"古之学者为己,今之学者为人。"

宪问第十四　Chapter Fourteen

蘧伯玉的使者说："我们先生想尽量减少过错却还未能做到。"

Qu Boyu's envoy said, "My master has been trying to reduce his mistakes, but has not achieved that yet."

14.25　蘧伯玉使人于孔子。孔子与之坐而问焉，曰："夫子何为？"对曰："夫子欲寡其过而未能也。"

使者出。子曰："使乎！使乎！"

【释义】

蘧伯玉派使者拜访孔子。孔子跟他同坐，并且问道："你们先生在做什么？"回答说："我们先生想尽量减少过错却还未能做到。"

使者出去以后，孔子说："难得的使者啊！难得的使者啊！"

【英译】

Qu Boyu sent an envoy to the Master. The Master sat with him and asked, "What has your master been doing?" The envoy answered, "My master has been trying to reduce his mistakes, but has not achieved that yet."

After the envoy left, the Master remarked, "What an excellent envoy! What an excellent envoy!"

Chapter Fourteen 宪问第十四

孔子说："不居某一职位，不考虑那方面的政事。"

The Master said, "Do not concern yourself with things that are not within the range of your responsibility."

14.26
zǐ yuē　　bú zài qí wèi　　bù móu qí zhèng
子曰："不在其位，不谋其政。"
zēng zǐ yuē　　jūn zǐ sī bù chū qí wèi
曾子曰："君子思不出其位。"

【释义】

孔子说："不居某一职位，不考虑那方面的政事。"

曾子说："君子考虑问题不越出自己的职权范围。"

【英译】

The Master said, "Do not concern yourself with things that are not within the range of your responsibility."

Zeng Zi said, "A man of virtue does not concern himself with things beyond the range of his responsibility."

宪问第十四　Chapter Fourteen

孔子说："君子以口里说的超过实际做的为耻。"

The Master said, "A man of virtue considers it shameful to say more and do fewer deeds."

【释义】

　　孔子说："君子以口里说的超过实际做的为耻。"

【英译】

　　The Master said, "A man of virtue considers it shameful to say more and do fewer deeds."

14.27 zǐ yuē　　jūn zǐ chǐ qí yán ér guò qí xíng
子曰："君子耻其言而过其行。"

Chapter Fourteen   宪问第十四

孔子说："有仁德的人不忧愁，有智慧的人不迷惑，勇敢的人不畏惧。"

The Master said, "Being virtuous, a man of virtue is free from worries; being wise, he is not confused; and being courageous, he does not have fears."

14.28
zǐ yuē　　jūn zǐ dào zhě sān　　wǒ wú néng yān　　rén zhě bù yōu
子曰："君子道者三，我无能焉：仁者不忧，
zhì zhě bú huò　　yǒng zhě bú jù　　zǐ gòng yuē　　fū zǐ zì
知者不惑，勇者不惧。"子贡曰："夫子自
dào yě
道也。"

【释义】

孔子说："君子之道有三，我没有能力做到，这就是：有仁德的人不忧愁，有智慧的人不迷惑，勇敢的人不畏惧。"子贡曰："这正是先生在说自己呢。"

【英译】

The Master said, "There are three aspects about a man of virtue, of which I have achieved none. Being virtuous, he is free from worries; being wise, he is not confused; and being courageous, he does not have fears." Zi Gong said, "This is an exact description of yourself, sir."

125

宪问第十四　Chapter Fourteen

子贡经常批评人。孔子说:"赐啊,你就比别人强吗?"

Zi Gong often leveled criticism at other people. The Master said, "Ci, can you guarantee that you are better than others?"

14.29 zǐ gòng bàng rén　zǐ yuē　cì yě xián hū zāi　fú wǒ zé bù xiá
子贡方人。子曰:"赐也贤乎哉?夫我则不暇。"

【释义】

子贡经常批评人。孔子说:"赐啊,你就比别人强吗?要是我就没有这样的闲工夫。"

【英译】

Zi Gong often leveled criticism at other people. The Master said, "Ci, can you guarantee that you are better than others? For me, I just can't find the time to do that."

Chapter Fourteen 宪问第十四

孔子说:"不忧虑别人不了解自己,忧虑自己没有能力。"

The Master said, "Do not worry about other people's ignorance of your capabilities; rather, worry about your own incapability."

【释义】

孔子说:"不忧虑别人不了解自己,忧虑自己没有能力。"

【英译】

The Master said, "Do not worry about other people's ignorance of your capabilities; rather, worry about your own incapability."

14.30
zǐ yuē　　　bú huàn rén zhī bù jǐ zhī　huàn qí bù néng yě
子曰:"不患人之不己知,患其不能也。"

宪问第十四　Chapter Fourteen

孔子说："不预先揣度别人的欺诈，不凭空猜测别人的不诚实，却又能及早发觉欺诈与不诚实，这样的人该是贤者吧？"

The Master said, "He who does not suspect others of cheating or doubt others' honesty on groundless presumptions yet is able to perceive problems beforehand can be called a sage."

【释义】

孔子说："不预先揣度别人的欺诈，不凭空猜测别人的不诚实，却又能及早发觉欺诈与不诚实，这样的人该是贤者吧？"

【英译】

The Master said, "He who does not suspect others of cheating or doubt others' honesty on groundless presumptions yet is able to perceive problems beforehand can be called a sage."

14.31　zǐ yuē　bú nì zhà　bú yì bú xìn　yì yì xiān jué zhě　shì
子曰："不逆诈，不亿不信，抑亦先觉者，是
xián hū
贤乎！"

Chapter Fourteen 宪问第十四

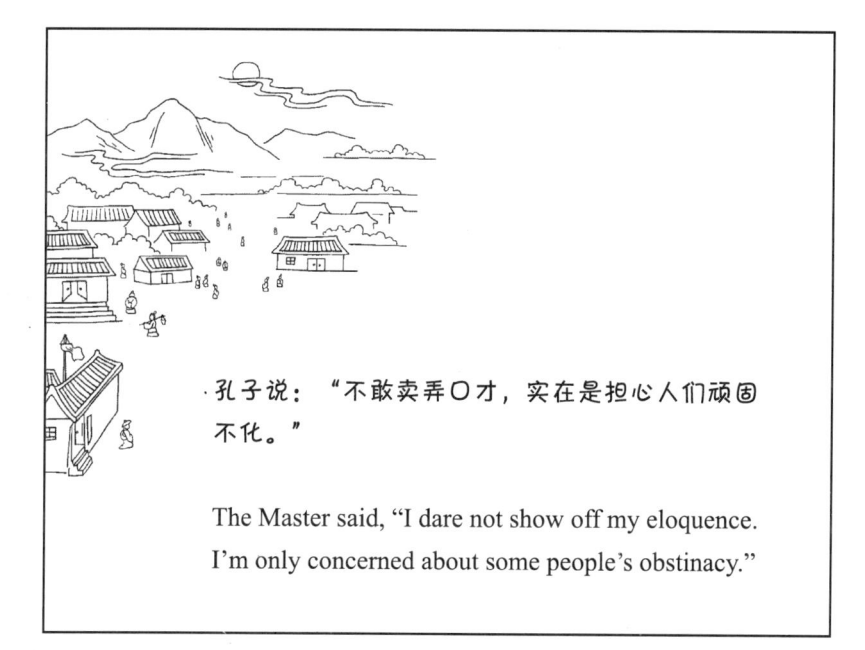

孔子说："不敢卖弄口才，实在是担心人们顽固不化。"

The Master said, "I dare not show off my eloquence. I'm only concerned about some people's obstinacy."

14.32
wēi shēng mǔ wèi kǒng zǐ yuē　　qiū hé wéi shì xī xī zhě yú　　wú nǎi
微 生 亩 谓 孔 子 曰："丘 何 为 是 栖 栖 者 与？无 乃
wéi nìng hū　　kǒng zǐ yuē　　fēi gǎn wéi nìng yě　　jí gù yě
为 佞 乎？" 孔 子 曰："非 敢 为 佞 也，疾 固 也。"

【释义】

微生亩对孔子说："你孔丘为什么要这样遑遑不安到处游说呢？不会是要卖弄口才吧？"孔子说："不敢卖弄口才，实在是担心人们顽固不化。"

【英译】

Weisheng Mu (a hermit in the Lu State) asked the Master, "Why are you hurrying around selling your ideas? Is it for the purpose of showing off your eloquence?" The Master answered, "I dare not show off my eloquence. I'm only concerned about some people's obstinacy."

129

宪问第十四　Chapter Fourteen

【释义】

孔子说:"对于好马,不是称赞它的气力,而是称赞它的美德。"

【英译】

The Master said, "A good steed is praised for its virtue, not its strength."

孔子说:"对于好马,不是称赞它的气力,而是称赞它的美德。"

The Master said, "A good steed is praised for its virtue, not its strength."

14.33　zǐ yuē　　jì bù chēng qí lì　chēng qí dé yě
子曰:"骥不称其力,称其德也。"

Chapter Fourteen 宪问第十四

孔子说："用正直来回报怨恨，用恩德来回报恩德。"

The Master said, "Repay harm with justice, and repay good with good."

【释义】

有人说："用恩德来回报怨恨，怎么样？"孔子说："那用什么来回报恩德呢？应该是用正直来回报怨恨，用恩德来回报恩德。"

【英译】

Someone asked, "What do you think of the saying of 'Repay harm with good'?" The Master answered, "Then with what should one repay good? Therefore, repay harm with justice, and repay good with good."

14.34
huò yuē　　　yǐ dé bào yuàn　hé rú　　　zǐ yuē　　hé yǐ bào
或曰："以德报怨，何如？"子曰："何以报
dé　　yǐ zhí bào yuàn　yǐ dé bào dé
德？以直报怨，以德报德。"

宪问第十四　Chapter Fourteen

【释义】

孔子说："没有人了解我啊！"子贡说："为什么没有人了解您呢？"孔子说："不怨恨上天，不责怪别人，身居下位老老实实学习，就会上通于天。了解我的大概是上天吧？"

【英译】

The Master said, "No one understands me." Zi Gong asked, "Why so?" The Master answered, "I bear no resentment against Heaven, and I do not complain about people. From a humble origin I have studied hard and have got an understanding of Heaven. Perhaps Heaven alone understands me."

孔子说："不怨恨上天，不责怪别人，身居下位老老实实学习，就会上通于天，了解我的大概是上天吧？"

The Master said, "I bear no resentment against Heaven, and I do not complain about people. From a humble origin I have studied hard and have got an understanding of Heaven. Perhaps Heaven alone understands me."

14.35

zǐ yuē　　　mò wǒ zhī yě fú　　　zǐ gòng yuē　　　hé wéi qí mò
子曰："莫我知也夫！"子贡曰："何为其莫
zhī zǐ yě　　　zǐ yuē　　　bú yuàn tiān　　　bù yóu rén　　　xià xué ér
知子也？"子曰："不怨天，不尤人，下学而
shàng dá　　　zhī wǒ zhě qí tiān hū
上　达。知我者其天乎！"

Chapter Fourteen 宪问第十四

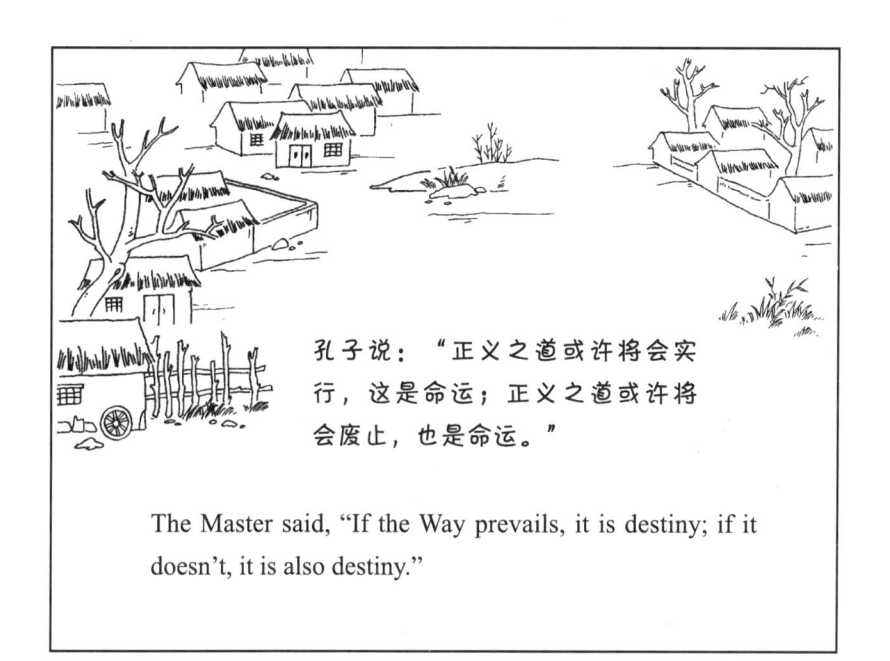

孔子说："正义之道或许将会实行，这是命运；正义之道或许将会废止，也是命运。"

The Master said, "If the Way prevails, it is destiny; if it doesn't, it is also destiny."

14.36

gōng bó liáo sù zǐ lù yú jì sūn   zǐ fú jǐng bó yǐ gào   yuē   fū
公 伯 寮 愬 子 路 于 季 孙。子 服 景 伯 以 告，曰："夫

zǐ gù yǒu huò zhì yú gōng bó liáo   wú lì yóu néng sì zhū shì cháo
子 固 有 惑 志 于 公 伯 寮，吾 力 犹 能 肆 诸 市 朝。"

zǐ yuē   dào zhī jiāng xíng yě yú   mìng yě   dào zhī jiāng fèi yě yú
子 曰："道 之 将 行 也 与，命 也；道 之 将 废 也 与，

mìng yě   gōng bó liáo qí rú mìng hé
命 也。公 伯 寮 其 如 命 何？"

【释义】

公伯寮向季孙诬告子路。子服景伯把这件事告诉了孔子，并且说："季孙这位先生已经被公伯寮迷惑了，可是我的力量还足能把他杀了陈尸街头。"

孔子说："正义之道或许将会实行，这是命运；正义之道或许将会废止，也是命运。公伯寮他能把命运怎么样呢？"

【英译】

Gongbo Liao spoke ill of Zi Lu to Ji Sun, the lord they both served. Zifu Jingbo told the Master about this and added, "Lord Ji has already shown signs of distrust of Zi Lu, but I still have enough power to kill Gongbo Liao and have his body displayed in the market."

The Master answered, "If the Way prevails, it is destiny; if it doesn't, it is also destiny. What can Gongbo Liao do with destiny?"

宪问第十四　Chapter Fourteen

孔子说："贤者以避开乱世为上策，其次避开乱地，再次避开傲色，再次避开恶言。"

The Master said, "For wise people, those who shun chaotic society come first; those who shun chaotic places come next; those who shun arrogant looks come third; and those who shun hostile words come last."

14.37
zǐ yuē　xián zhě bì shì　qí cì bì dì　qí cì bì sè　qí
子曰："贤者辟世，其次辟地，其次辟色，其
cì bì yán
次辟言。"
zǐ yuē　zuò zhě qī rén yǐ
子曰："作者七人矣。"

【释义】

孔子说："贤者以避开乱世为上策，其次避开乱地，再次避开傲色，再次避开恶言。"

孔子又说："做到这样的已经有七个人了。"

【英译】

The Master said, "For wise people, those who shun chaotic society come first; those who shun chaotic places come next; those who shun arrogant looks come third; and those who shun hostile words come last."

He then added, "There are already seven people who have achieved this."

Chapter Fourteen 宪问第十四

守门人说："此人就是那个明知行不通却硬要去做的人吗？"

The gatekeeper said, "Is this the man who persists in doing what he knows is impossible?"

14.38 子路宿于石门。晨门曰："奚自？"子路曰："自孔氏。"曰："是知其不可而为之者与？"

【释义】

子路在石门过夜。守城门的人说："从哪里来？"子路说："从孔氏那里来。"守门人说："此人就是那个明知行不通却硬要去做的人吗？"

【英译】

Zi Lu stayed overnight at the Stone Gate. The gatekeeper asked, "Where are you from?" Zi Lu answered, "From the household of Confucius." The gatekeeper asked, "Is this the man who persists in doing what he knows is impossible?"

宪问第十四　Chapter Fourteen

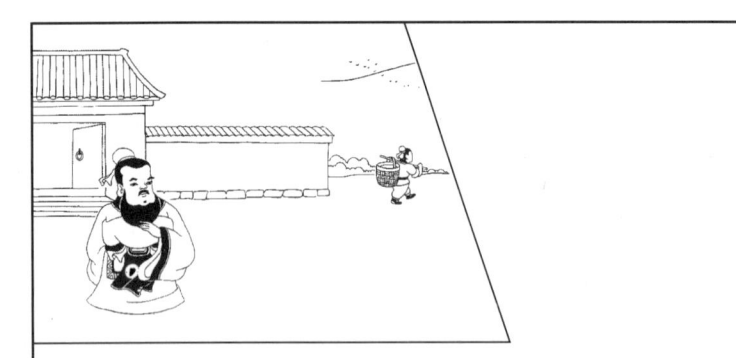

孔子说："好坚决啊！没有什么可责问他的了。"

The Master said, "He surely sounds resolute! There seems to be no argument against him."

14.39

zǐ jī qìng yú wèi　　yǒu hè kuì ér guò kǒng shì zhī mén zhě　yuē　yǒu
子击磬于卫。有荷蒉而过孔氏之门者，曰："有
xīn zāi　　jī qìng hū　　jì ér yuē　　bǐ zāi　kēng kēng hū
心哉，击磬乎！"既而曰："鄙哉，硁硁乎！
mò jǐ zhī yě　　sī jǐ ér yǐ yǐ　　shēn zé lì　qiǎn zé jiē
莫己知也，斯己而已矣。'深则厉，浅则揭。'"
zǐ yuē　　guǒ zāi　　mò zhī nàn yǐ
子曰："果哉！末之难矣。"

【释义】

孔子在卫国击磬，有个身背土筐路过孔子门前的人，说："有心啊，这个击磬的人！"过了一会儿又说："褊狭啊，硁硁的磬声透着固执！没有人了解自己，就专己守志算了。《诗经》说得好：'河深就穿着衣裳过，河浅就提起衣裳过。'"孔子说："好坚决啊！没有什么可责问他的了。"

【英译】

One day while in the State of Wei, the Master was playing the stone chimes. A man carrying a basket on his back was passing by and said, "The man playing the chimes must have his own idea!" After a while, he added, "He is surely stubborn! This I can tell by listening to the sound of his chimes. If no one understands you, just let it be. As is said in *The Book of Songs*, 'If the river is deep, just wade across; if the river is shallow, lift your robe and keep it dry.'" The Master said, "He surely sounds resolute! There seems to be no argument against him."

Chapter Fourteen 宪问第十四

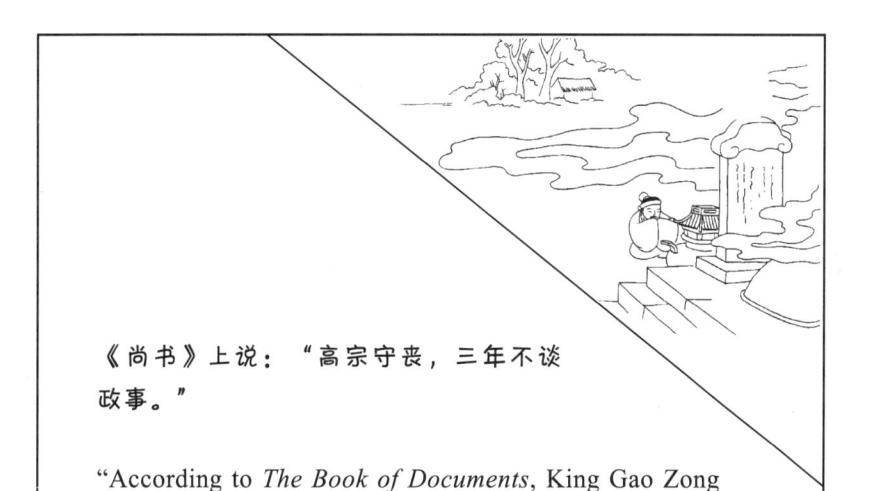

《尚书》上说："高宗守丧，三年不谈政事。"

"According to *The Book of Documents*, King Gao Zong remained in mourning for his father for three years, during which period he stayed away from government affairs."

14.40
zǐ zhāng yuē　　　shū yún　　gāo zōng liàng yīn　sān nián bù yán
子张曰："《书》云：'高宗谅阴，三年不言。'
hé wèi yě　　　zǐ yuē　　　hé bì gāo zōng　gǔ zhī rén jiē rán
何谓也？"子曰："何必高宗，古之人皆然。
jūn hōng　bǎi guān zǒng jǐ　yǐ tīng yú zhǒng zǎi sān nián
君薨，百官总己以听于冢宰三年。"

【释义】

子张说："《尚书》上说：'高宗守丧，三年不谈政事。'这是什么意思？"孔子说："不仅高宗，古代的人都这样。国君死了，朝廷百官都总管自己的职事，并听命于冢宰三年。"

【英译】

Zi Zhang said, "According to *The Book of Historical Documents*, King Gao Zong remained in mourning for his father for three years, during which period he stayed away from government affairs. What does this mean?" The Master answered, "In ancient times, all people followed this practice, and Gao Zong was no exception. When a sovereign died, the successor would remain in mourning for three years, and during this period all the officials in court would serve under the command of the chief minister."

137

宪问第十四　Chapter Fourteen

【释义】

孔子说："居上位的人喜好礼，那么老百姓就容易役使。"

【英译】

The Master said, "When people in high positions are willing to observe etiquette, then it will be easy to use the labor of the common people."

孔子说："居上位的人喜好礼，那么老百姓就容易役使。"

The Master said, "When people in high positions are willing to observe etiquette, then it will be easy to use the labor of the common people."

14.41

zǐ yuē　　shàng hào lǐ　　zé mín yì shǐ yě
子曰："上好礼，则民易使也。"

Chapter Fourteen　宪问第十四

孔子说："修养自己而敬慎从事；修养自己而安抚别人；修养自己而安定百姓。"

The Master said, "Conduct self-cultivation and be prudent in doing things; conduct self-cultivation and try to comfort and placate others; conduct self-cultivation and bring peace and stability to the common people."

14:42

zǐ lù wèn jūn zǐ。 zǐ yuē： xiū jǐ yǐ jìng。 yuē： rú
子路问君子。子曰："修己以敬。"曰："如
sī ér yǐ hū？ yuē xiū jǐ yǐ ān rén。 yuē： rú
斯而已乎？"曰："修己以安人。"曰："如
sī ér yǐ hū？ yuē xiū jǐ yǐ ān bǎi xìng。 xiū jǐ yǐ ān
斯而已乎？"曰："修己以安百姓。修己以安
bǎi xìng， yáo shùn qí yóu bìng zhū！
百姓，尧舜其犹病诸！"

【释义】

子路问什么是君子。孔子说："修养自己而敬慎从事。"又问："这样就够了吗？"孔子说："修养自己而安抚别人。"又问："这样就够了吗？"孔子说："修养自己而安定百姓。修养自己而安定百姓，就连尧舜恐怕还要为此犯难呢！"

【英译】

Zi Lu asked how to become a man of virtue. The Master answered, "Conduct self-cultivation and be prudent in doing things." Zi Lu asked, "Is this enough?" The Master answered, "Conduct self-cultivation and try to comfort and placate others." Zi Lu asked again, "Is this enough?" The Master answered, "Conduct self-cultivation and bring peace and stability to the common people. Even for the ancient sage kings Yao and Shun, this is hard to achieve."

139

宪问第十四 Chapter Fourteen

原壤坐无坐相,放肆地等待孔子。孔子说:"幼小时就不谦逊敬长,长大了又无所传述,老朽了还不快死,这简直是祸害!"说完,用手杖敲了敲他的小腿。

While waiting for Confucius, Yuan Rang sat improperly. The Master remarked, "When you were a child, you were not respectful to your elders; when you grew up, you had achieved nothing; and now you are in your old age, you refuse to die. You are truly a pest!" With that, the Master tapped the shin of the old man with his stick.

【释义】

原壤坐无坐相,放肆地等待孔子。孔子说:"幼小时就不谦逊敬长,长大了又无所传述,老朽了还不快死,这简直是祸害!"说完,用手杖敲了敲他的小腿。"

【英译】

While waiting for Confucius, Yuan Rang sat improperly. The Master remarked, "When you were a child, you were not respectful to your elders; when you grew up, you had achieved nothing; and now you are in your old age, you refuse to die. You are truly a pest!" With that, the Master tapped the shin of the old man with his stick.

14.43 yuán rǎng yí sì。zǐ yuē:"yòu ér bú xùn tì,zhǎng ér wú shù
原 壤 夷 俟。子 曰:"幼 而 不 孙 弟,长 而 无 述
yān,lǎo ér bù sǐ,shì wéi zéi！" yǐ zhàng kòu qí jìng。
焉,老 而 不 死,是 为 贼！"以 杖 叩 其 胫。

Chapter Fourteen 宪问第十四

孔子说:"阙党少年不是一个追求进步的人,而是一个贪图速成的人。"

The Master said, "What the young man is after is not progress in learning, but quick success."

14.44
què dǎng tóng zǐ jiāng mìng。huò wèn zhī yuē: "yì zhě yú?" zǐ yuē:
阙党童子将命。或问之曰:"益者与?"子曰:
wú jiàn qí jū yú wèi yě, jiàn qí yǔ xiān shēng bìng xíng yě。 fēi qiú
"吾见其居于位也,见其与先生并行也。非求
yì zhě yě, yù sù chéng zhě yě。
益者也,欲速成者也。"

【释义】

阙党的一个少年负责为宾主传达言语。有人问起他,说:"是个有长进的后生吗?"孔子说:"我见他忝居成人之位,又见他与年长者并肩而行。可知他不是一个追求进步的人,而是一个贪图速成的人。"

【英译】

A young man from the Village Que worked as a messenger between hosts and guests. Someone asked, "Is the young man likely to make progress?" The Master answered, "I saw him taking seat for an adult and walking alongside his seniors. Obviously what he is after is not progress in learning, but quick success."

wèi líng gōng dì shí wǔ
卫灵公第十五
CHAPTER FIFTEEN

Chapter Fifteen 卫灵公第十五

孔子说:"礼仪的事情,我曾经听到过;军队的事情,却未曾学习过。"

The Master said, "I have learned about etiquette and rituals, but I have never studied military affairs."

【释义】

卫灵公向孔子询问作战的阵法。孔子答道:"礼仪的事情,我曾经听到过;军队的事情,却未曾学习过。"第二天便动身离开了卫国。

【英译】

Duke Ling of the Wei State asked Confucius about combat tactics. The Master answered, "I have learned about etiquette and rituals, but I have never studied military affairs." The very next day, he left Wei.

15.1
wèi líng gōng wèn zhèn yú kǒng zǐ　　kǒng zǐ duì yuē　　　zǔ dòu zhī shì
卫 灵 公 问 陈 于 孔 子。孔 子 对 曰:"俎 豆 之 事,
zé cháng wén zhī yǐ　　jūn lǚ zhī shì　　wèi zhī xué yě　　　míng rì suì
则 尝 闻 之 矣;军 旅 之 事,未 之 学 也。"明 日 遂
xíng
行。

卫灵公第十五　Chapter Fifteen

孔子说："君子安于穷困，小人遇到穷困，就会胡作非为了。"

The Master said, "Men of virtue remain unperturbed even in the face of hardships. In contrast, petty-minded men would stop at nothing when facing a similar situation."

15.2
zài chén jué liáng, cóng zhě bìng, mò néng xīng。zǐ lù yùn jiàn yuē:
在陈绝粮，从者病，莫能兴。子路愠见曰：
jūn zǐ yì yǒu qióng hū? zǐ yuē: jūn zǐ gù qióng, xiǎo
"君子亦有穷乎？"子曰："君子固穷，小
rén qióng sī làn yǐ。
人穷斯滥矣。"

【释义】

孔子在陈国断绝了粮食，跟从的人都饿坏了，没有人能爬得起来。子路带着满腔愤怨来见孔子说："君子也有穷困的时候吗？"孔子说："君子安于穷困，小人遇到穷困，就会胡作非为了。"

【英译】

When in the State of Chen, the Master had run out of food. His disciples were so starved that they could not even stand up. Angry and resentful, Zi Lu came to see his teacher and asked, "Do men of virtue have to suffer such hardships?" The Master answered, "Men of virtue remain unperturbed even in the face of hardships. In contrast, petty-minded men would stop at nothing when facing a similar situation."

Chapter Fifteen 卫灵公第十五

孔子说："我是用一个基本内容把它们贯穿起来的。"

The Master said, "What I do is using a core thread to bind everything together."

15.3
zǐ yuē　　　　cì yě　　rǔ yǐ yú wéi duō xué ér zhì zhī zhě yú
子曰："赐也，女以予为多学而识之者与？"
duì yuē　　rán　fēi yú　　yuē　　fēi yě　　yú yī yǐ guàn
对曰："然，非与？"曰："非也，予一以贯
zhī
之。"

【释义】

孔子说："赐，你以为我是多方面学习并且一一把内容强记下来的吗？"子贡回答说："是的，难道不是吗？"孔子说："不是的，我是用一个基本内容把它们贯穿起来的。"

【英译】

The Master said, "Ci, Do you think I learn extensively and then manage to remember everything?" His disciple answered, "Yes, I do. Isn't it so?" The Master said, "No, what I do is using a core thread to bind everything together."

145

卫灵公第十五　Chapter Fifteen

孔子说："由，懂得道德的人太少了啊！"

The Master said, "You (Zi Lu), how few there are people who understand virtue!"

【释义】

孔子说："由，懂得道德的人太少了啊！"

【英译】

The Master said, "You (Zi Lu), how few there are people who understand virtue!"

15.4 zǐ yuē　yóu　zhī dé zhě xiǎn yǐ
子曰："由，知德者鲜矣。"

Chapter Fifteen 卫灵公第十五

孔子说："能够无所烦劳就能使天下大治的人大概就是舜吧。"

The Master said, "Shun must have been the only ruler who achieved good governance without exertion."

【释义】

孔子说："能够无所烦劳就能使天下大治的人大概就是舜吧。他做了什么呢？修养好自己，居位听政罢了。"

【英译】

The Master said, "Shun must have been the only ruler who achieved good governance without exertion. What did he do? Nothing but practicing self-cultivation and sitting in his royal seat."

15.5
zǐ yuē wú wéi ér zhì zhě qí shùn yě yú fú hé wéi zāi
子曰："无为而治者，其舜也与？夫何为哉？
gōng jǐ zhèng nán miàn ér yǐ yǐ
恭己正南面而已矣。"

卫灵公第十五　Chapter Fifteen

孔子说："说话要忠诚守信，行为要厚道慎重。"

The Master said, "Be sincere and honest in words, and be respectful and cautious in action."

15.6

zǐ zhāng wèn xíng　　zǐ yuē　　yán zhōng xìn　xíng dǔ jìng　　suī mán mò
子张问行。子曰："言忠信，行笃敬，虽蛮貊
zhī bāng　xíng yǐ　　yán bù zhōng xìn　xíng bù dǔ jìng　　suī zhōu lǐ
之邦，行矣。言不忠信，行不笃敬，虽州里，
xíng hū zāi　　lì　zé jiàn qí cān yú qián yě　　zài yú　zé jiàn qí
行乎哉？立，则见其参于前也；在舆，则见其
yǐ yú héng yě　　fú rán hòu xíng　　zǐ zhāng shū zhū shēn
倚于衡也。夫然后行。"子张书诸绅。

【释义】

子张问怎样才能在社会上行得通。孔子说："说话忠诚守信，行为厚道慎重，即使在落后部族的国家也能行得通。说话不忠诚守信，行为不厚道慎重，即使在本乡本土，又能行得通吗？站立时仿佛看见'忠信笃敬'这四个字就在前面；坐在车中仿佛看见这四个字就在车辕的横木上。能够做到这样，才能行得通。"子张把这段话写在了腰间的衣带上。

【英译】

Zi Zhang asked about how to get along in society. The Master said, "Be sincere and honest in words, and be respectful and cautious in action. If you can do this, you will get along even in remote and backward tribes. But if you do the opposite, you won't be able to get along even in your hometown. Wherever you are, whatever you do, always bear in mind these principles and act accordingly. Then you will get along in society." Zi Zhang wrote down these words on his sash.

Chapter Fifteen 卫灵公第十五

孔子说："国家政治清明，就出来做官；国家政治混乱，就辞退官职，把自己的主张藏在心里。"

The Master said, "When the Way prevailed, he chose to be a government official; when the Way did not prevail any more, he chose to retire and live in seclusion."

15.7
zǐ yuē zhí zāi shǐ yú bāng yǒu dào rú shǐ bāng wú dào
子曰："直哉，史鱼！邦有道，如矢；邦无道，
rú shǐ jūn zǐ zāi qú bó yù bāng yǒu dào zé shì bāng wú
如矢。君子哉，蘧伯玉！邦有道，则仕；邦无
dào zé kě juǎn ér huái zhī
道，则可卷而怀之。"

【释义】

孔子说："史鱼真是正直啊！国家政治清明，他的言行像箭一样直；国家政治混乱，他的言行也像箭一样直。蘧伯玉真是一位君子啊！国家政治清明，就出来做官；国家政治混乱，就辞退官职，把自己的主张藏在心里。

【英译】

The Master said, "Shi Yu is a man of integrity! When the Way prevailed in his state, he was as straight as an arrow; when the Way failed to prevail any more, he was still as straight as an arrow. Qu Boyu is a man of virtue! When the Way prevailed in his state, he chose to be a government official; when the Way did not prevail any more, he chose to retire and live in seclusion."

卫灵公第十五　Chapter Fifteen

孔子说："有智慧的人既不失去朋友，又不说错话。"

The Master said, "A man of wisdom neither loses friends nor wastes words."

15.8

zǐ yuē　　kě yǔ yán ér bù yǔ zhī yán　　shī rén　　bù kě yǔ yán
子曰："可与言而不与之言，失人；不可与言
ér yǔ zhī yán　　shī yán　　zhì zhě bù shī rén　　yì bù shī yán
而与之言，失言。知者不失人，亦不失言。"

【释义】

孔子说："可以同他谈话却不同他谈，这就是失掉了朋友；不可以同他谈话却同他谈，这就是说错了话。有智慧的人既不失去朋友，又不说错话。"

【英译】

The Master said, "To fail to speak to someone who is worthy of the conversation is to lose a friend; to speak to someone who is not worthy of the conversation is to waste words. A man of wisdom neither loses friends nor wastes words."

Chapter Fifteen 卫灵公第十五

孔子说："志士仁人，没有贪生怕死而损害仁的，只有牺牲自己的性命来成全仁的。"

The Master said, "For people of virtue and lofty ideals, there have never been a case of seeking to live at the expense of virtue, but there are cases of sacrificing lives to safeguard virtue."

【释义】

孔子说："志士仁人，没有贪生怕死而损害仁的，只有牺牲自己的性命来成全仁的。"

【英译】

The Master said, "For people of virtue and lofty ideals, there have never been a case of seeking to live at the expense of virtue, but there are cases of sacrificing lives to safeguard virtue."

15.9 子曰："志士仁人，无求生以害仁，有杀身以成仁。"

卫灵公第十五　Chapter Fifteen

孔子说："工人要想把活儿做好，首先必须使工具锋利。"

The Master said, "For a craftsman, if he wants to do his work well, he has to sharpen his tools first."

15.10
zǐ gòng wèn wéi rén　　zǐ yuē　　gōng yù shàn qí shì　　bì xiān lì
子贡问为仁。子曰："工欲善其事，必先利
qí qì　　jū shì bāng yě　　shì qí dà fū zhī xián zhě　　yǒu qí shì
其器。居是邦也，事其大夫之贤者，友其士
zhī rén zhě
之仁者。"

【释义】

子贡问如何修养仁德。孔子说："工人要想把活儿做好，首先必须使工具锋利。住在这个国家，就要侍奉大夫中的那些贤者，与士人中的仁者交朋友。"

【英译】

Zi Gong asked about the cultivation of virtue. The Master said, "For a craftsman, if he wants to do his work well, he has to sharpen his tools first. Whichever state you are in, serve the virtuous among the ministers and befriend the humane among the scholars."

Chapter Fifteen 卫灵公第十五

颜渊问怎样治国。孔子说:"用夏代的历法,乘殷代的车子,戴周代的礼帽,音乐则用舜时的《韶舞》。"

Yan Yuan asked about ways to govern a state. The Master answered, "Follow the Calendar of the Xia Dynasty, ride the chariots of the Yin Dynasty, and wear the ceremonial hats of the Zhou Dynasty. As for music, adopt the *Shao* and *Wu*, which was played during the reign of Shun."

15.11
yán yuān wèn wéi bāng　　zǐ yuē　　xíng xià zhī shí　 chéng yīn zhī lù
颜渊问为邦。子曰:"行夏之时,乘殷之辂,
fú zhōu zhī miǎn　　 yuè zé sháo wǔ　　fàng zhèng shēng　yuǎn nìng rén
服周之冕,乐则《韶舞》。放郑声,远佞人。
zhèng shēng yín　　nìng rén dài
郑 声 淫,佞人殆。"

【释义】

颜渊问怎样治国。孔子说:"用夏代的历法,乘殷代的车子,戴周代的礼帽,音乐则用舜时的《韶舞》。排斥郑国的乐曲,远离花言巧语的人。郑国的乐曲过分,花言巧语的人危险。"

【英译】

Yan Yuan asked about ways to govern a state. The Master answered, "Follow the Calendar of the Xia Dynasty, ride the chariots of the Yin Dynasty, and wear the ceremonial hats of the Zhou Dynasty. As for music, adopt the *Shao* and *Wu*, which was played during the reign of Shun. Banish the music of Zheng and stay away from petty men of flattery words, because the music of Zheng is lustful and petty men of flattery words are dangerous."

153

卫灵公第十五　Chapter Fifteen

孔子说："一个人如果没有长远的考虑，一定会有眼前的忧患。"

The Master said, "A man who gives no thoughts to future happenings is sure to be beset by worries close at hand."

15.12
zǐ yuē　　rén wú yuǎn lǜ　　bì yǒu jìn yōu
子曰："人无远虑，必有近忧。"

【释义】

孔子说："一个人如果没有长远的考虑，一定会有眼前的忧患。"

【英译】

The Master said, "A man who gives no thoughts to future happenings is sure to be beset by worries close at hand."

Chapter Fifteen 卫灵公第十五

孔子说："罢了！我没有见过能像爱好女色那样爱好仁德的人。"

The Master said, "It is hopeless! I have never seen a man loving virtue as much as he loves women."

【释义】

孔子说："罢了！我没有见过能像爱好女色那样爱好仁德的人。"

【英译】

The Master said, "It is hopeless! I have never seen a man loving virtue as much as he loves women."

15.13
zǐ yuē　　　yǐ yǐ hū　wú wèi jiàn hào dé rú hào sè zhě yě
子曰："已矣乎！吾未见好德如好色者也。"

卫灵公第十五　Chapter Fifteen

The Master said, "Zang Wenzhong seemed an unqualified official who was jealous of others' worth and ability. He knew the virtue and talent of Liuxia Hui, yet he did not recommend him for an official post to work along with him."

15.14
zǐ yuē　zāng wén zhòng　qí qiè wèi zhě yú　zhī liǔ xià huì zhī xián
子曰："臧文仲，其窃位者与？知柳下惠之贤，
ér bù yǔ lì yě
而不与立也。"

【释义】

孔子说："臧文仲大概是个嫉贤妒能、窃居官位的人吧？明知柳下惠有贤德却不推举他跟自己并立于朝一起做官。"

【英译】

The Master said, "Zang Wenzhong seemed an unqualified official who was jealous of other's worth and ability. He knew the virtue and talent of Liuxia Hui, yet he did not recommend him for an official post to work along with him."

Chapter Fifteen 卫灵公第十五

孔子说:"对自己要求严格而尽量少责怪别人,怨恨就会远离自己。"

The Master said, "He who is hard on himself but lenient to others will stay clear of resentment."

【释义】

孔子说:"对自己要求严格而尽量少责怪别人,怨恨就会远离自己。"

【英译】

The Master said, "He who is hard on himself but lenient to others will stay clear of resentment."

15.15
zǐ yuē　　gōng zì hòu ér bó zé yú rén　zé yuǎn yuàn yǐ
子曰:"躬自厚而薄则于人,则远怨矣。"

157

卫灵公第十五　Chapter Fifteen

孔子说："不念叨'怎么办、怎么办'的人,我不知拿他怎么办。"

The Master said, "For a man who never asks himself 'What should I do? What should I do?' I really do not know what to do with him."

【释义】

孔子说："不念叨'怎么办、怎么办'的人,我不知拿他怎么办。"

【英译】

The Master said, "For a man who never asks himself 'What should I do? What should I do?' I really do not know what to do with him."

15.16 子曰："不曰'如之何、如之何'者,吾末如之何也已矣。"

Chapter Fifteen 卫灵公第十五

孔子说:"士人整日相聚在一起,谈话丝毫不涉及道义,只喜欢卖弄小聪明,难以有所成啊!"

The Master said, "People who get together every day, talking about nothing related to virtue but just showing off their cleverness at trial matters, can hardly achieve anything."

【释义】

孔子说:"士人整日相聚在一起,谈话丝毫不涉及道义,只喜欢卖弄小聪明,难以有所成啊!"

【英译】

The Master said, "People who get together every day, talking about nothing related to virtue but just showing off their cleverness at trial matters, can hardly achieve anything."

15.17

zǐ yuē　　qún jū zhōng rì　　yán bù jí yì　　hào xíng xiǎo huì　　nán
子曰:"群居终日,言不及义,好行小慧,难
yǐ zāi
矣哉!"

卫灵公第十五　Chapter Fifteen

【释义】

孔子说："君子按照义来修养自己的品质，按照礼来行事，用谦逊的态度讲话，靠信实取得成功。这才是君子啊！"

【英译】

The Master said, "A man of virtue cultivates himself in accord with righteousness, acts in accord with etiquette, speaks in a humble manner, and achieves success through integrity and effort."

孔子说："君子按照义来修养自己的品质，按照礼来行事，用谦逊的态度讲话，靠信实取得成功。这才是君子啊！"

The Master said, "A man of virtue cultivates himself in accord with righteousness, acts in accord with etiquette, speaks in a humble manner, and achieves success through integrity and effort."

15.18

zǐ yuē　　　jūn zǐ yì yǐ wéi zhì　　lǐ yǐ xíng zhī　　xùn yǐ chū
子曰："君子义以为质，礼以行之，孙以出
zhī　　xìn yǐ chéng zhī　　jūn zǐ zāi
之，信以成之。君子哉！"

Chapter Fifteen 卫灵公第十五

孔子说："君子担忧自己没有本事，不担忧别人不了解自己。"

The Master said, "A man of virtue is concerned with the inadequacy of his capability, not with other people's ignorance if his capability."

【释义】

孔子说："君子担忧自己没有本事，不担忧别人不了解自己。"

【英译】

The Master said, "A man of virtue is concerned with the inadequacy of his capability, not with other people's ignorance of his capability."

15.19　zǐ yuē　jūn zǐ bìng wú néng yān　bú bìng rén zhī bù jǐ zhī yě
子曰："君子病无能焉，不病人之不己知也。"

卫灵公第十五　Chapter Fifteen

孔子说："君子疾恨自己死后名声不能流传后世。"

The Master said, "A man of virtue hates to leave the world without making a long lasting good reputation."

【释义】

孔子说："君子疾恨自己死后名声不能流传后世。"

【英译】

The Master said, "A man of virtue hates to leave the world without making a long lasting good reputation."

15.20 zǐ yuē　jūn zǐ　jí mò shì　ér míng bù chēng yān
子曰："君子疾没世而名不称焉。"

Chapter Fifteen　卫灵公第十五

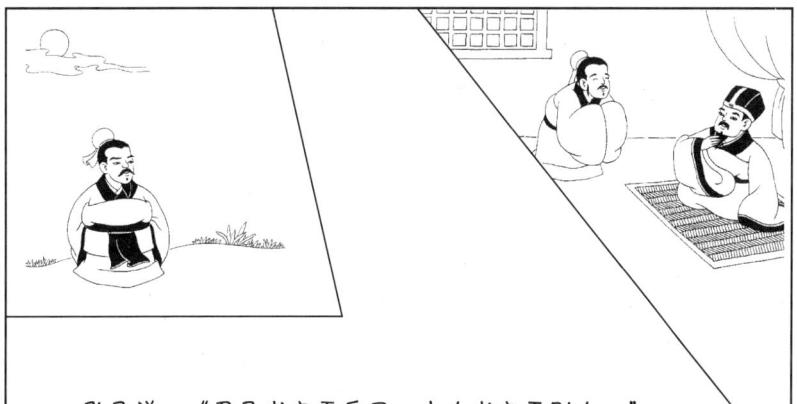

孔子说："君子求之于自己，小人求之于别人。"

The Master said, "A man of virtue depends on himself, while a petty-minded man depends on others."

【释义】

孔子说："君子求之于自己，小人求之于别人。"

【英译】

The Master said, "A man of virtue depends on himself, while a petty-minded man depends on others."

15.21　zǐ yuē　jūn zǐ qiú zhū jǐ　xiǎo rén qiú zhū rén
子曰："君子求诸己，小人求诸人。"

卫灵公第十五　Chapter Fifteen

孔子说："君子庄重自尊却不与人争,合群团结却不结党营私。"

The Master said, "A man of virtue is dignified and self-respecting, but not contentious. He gets along well with others, but never joins a clique to pursue material gains."

【释义】

孔子说："君子庄重自尊却不与人争,合群团结却不结党营私。"

【英译】

The Master said, "A man of virtue is dignified and self-respecting, but not contentious. He gets along well with others, but never joins a clique to pursue material gains."

15.22
zǐ yuē　jūn zǐ jīn ér bù zhēng　qún ér bù dǎng
子曰："君子矜而不争,群而不党。"

Chapter Fifteen 卫灵公第十五

孔子说："君子不根据言辞来选拔人，也不因为一个人不好而废弃他有价值的话。"

The Master said, "A man of virtue does not select a man on the basis of what he says, nor does he disregard the words of worth because it is said by an unworthy man."

【释义】

孔子说："君子不根据言辞来选拔人，也不因为一个人不好而废弃他有价值的话。"

【英译】

The Master said, "A man of virtue does not select a man on the basis of what he says, nor does he disregard the words of worth because it is said by an unworthy man."

15.23   zǐ yuē   jūn zǐ bù yǐ yán jǔ rén   bù yǐ rén fèi yán
子曰："君子不以言举人，不以人废言。"

165

卫灵公第十五　Chapter Fifteen

【释义】

子贡问道："有一个字可以终生遵照它去做吗？"孔子说："大概是'恕'吧。意思是自己不愿意的事情，不要强加给别人。"

【英译】

Zi Gong asked, "Is there a single word that one can follow during one's lifetime?" The Master answered, "It must be *shu*, meaning: do not impose on others what you yourself do not like."

孔子说："自己不愿意的事情，不要强加给别人。"

The Master said, "Do not impose on others what you yourself do not like."

15.24
zǐ gòng wèn yuē　　　yǒu yì yán ér　kě　yǐ zhōng shēn xíng zhī zhě hū
子贡问曰："有一言而可以终身行之者乎？"
zǐ yuē　　qí　shù　hū　jǐ suǒ bú yù　wù shī yú rén
子曰："其'恕'乎！己所不欲，勿施于人。"

Chapter Fifteen 卫灵公第十五

孔子说："我对于别人，诋毁过谁？称赞过谁？如果有称赞别人的情况，那一定是经过验证了的。"

The Master said, "In my contact with other people, whom did I speak ill of? And whom did I praise? If there are people I have praised, they have stood to test."

15.25
子曰："吾之于人也，谁毁谁誉？如有所誉者，其有所试矣。斯民也，三代之所以直道而行也。"

【释义】

孔子说："我对于别人，诋毁过谁？称赞过谁？如果有称赞别人的情况，那一定是经过验证了的。这样不被虚誉的人民，正是夏、商、周三代推行正直之道的依靠。"

【英译】

The Master said, "In my contact with other people, whom did I speak ill of? And whom did I praise? If there are people I have praised, they have stood to test. It was such people that the Three Dynasties (Xia, Shang, Zhou) relied on for the practice of the just rule."

167

卫灵公第十五　Chapter Fifteen

孔子说："我还看得到史书中因有疑问而空缺不记的情况，就像有马不能驾驭借给别人乘用一样。如今则没有这种情况了！"

The Master said, "I saw cases where parts of a historical document remained blank for further confirmation. There were also cases where a horse owner would let others to tame the horse before he could ride it. Nowadays there are no such cases any more."

15.26
zǐ yuē　　　　　wú yóu jí shǐ zhī quē wén yě　　yǒu mǎ zhě jiè rén chéng
子曰："吾犹及史之阙文也，有马者借人乘
zhī　 jīn wú yǐ fú
之。今亡矣夫！"

【释义】

孔子说："我还看得到史书中因有疑问而空缺不记的情况，就像有马不能驾驭借给别人乘用一样。如今则没有这种情况了！"

【英译】

The Master said, "I saw cases where parts of a historical document remained blank for further confirmation. There were also cases where a horse owner would let others to tame the horse before he could ride it. Nowadays there are no such cases any more."

Chapter Fifteen　卫灵公第十五

孔子说："花言巧语能惑乱道德。小事不忍耐就会打乱大的计谋。"

The Master said, "Flattery words does harm to virtue. Lack of forbearance in small matters will upset big plans."

【释义】

孔子说："花言巧语能惑乱道德。小事不忍耐就会打乱大的计谋。"

【英译】

The Master said, "Flattery words does harm to virtue. Lack of forbearance in small matters will upset big plans."

15.27
zǐ yuē　　qiǎo yán luàn dé　xiǎo bù rěn zé luàn dà móu
子曰："巧言乱德。小不忍则乱大谋。"

169

卫灵公第十五　Chapter Fifteen

【释义】

孔子说:"众人都厌恶他,一定要对他加以考察;众人都喜欢他,也一定要对他加以考察。"

【英译】

The Master said, "If a man is detested by all, then the case should be examined; if a man is liked by all, then the case should also be examined."

孔子说:"众人都厌恶他,一定要对他加以考察;众人都喜欢他,也一定要对他加以考察。"

The Master said, "If a man is detested by all, then the case should be examined; if a man is like by all, then the case should also be examined."

15.28 zǐ yuē　　zhòng wù zhī　bì chá yān　zhòng hào zhī　bì chá yān
子曰:"众 恶 之, 必 察 焉; 众 好 之, 必 察 焉。"

Chapter Fifteen　卫灵公第十五

孔子说：" 人能发扬光大道，不是道能光大人。"

The Master said, "Man can promote the Way, but the Way can not promote man."

【释义】

孔子说：" 人能发扬光大道，不是道能光大人。"

【英译】

The Master said, "Man can promote the Way, but the Way can not promote man."

15.29　zǐ yuē　　　rén néng hóng dào　　fēi dào hóng rén
子曰："人能弘道，非道弘人。"

171

卫灵公第十五　Chapter Fifteen

【释义】

孔子说:"犯了过错而不改正,这才叫做过错呢。"

【英译】

The Master said, "To make mistakes and not correct them is to make real mistakes."

孔子说:"犯了过错而不改正,这才叫做过错呢。"

The Master said, "To make mistakes and not correct them is to make real mistakes."

15.30
zǐ yuē　　guò ér bù gǎi　　shì wèi guò yǐ
子曰:"过而不改,是谓过矣。"

Chapter Fifteen 卫灵公第十五

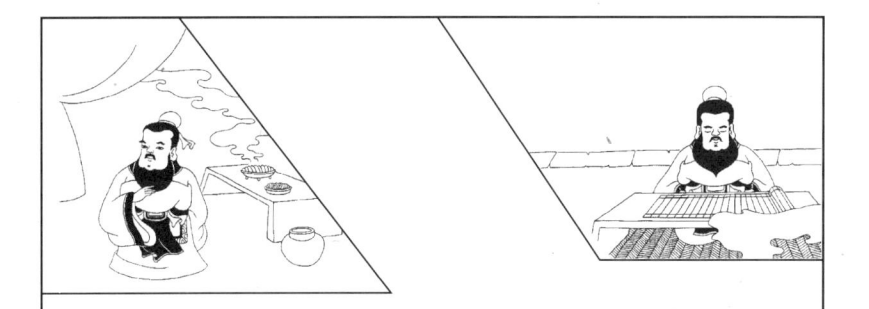

孔子说："我曾经整日不吃饭，整夜不睡觉，用来思考，结果没有获益，还不如学习为好呢。"

The Master said, "For a period, I spent the whole time thinking without eating any food nor taking any sleep, but to no avail. It would have been better if I had spent the time learning."

【释义】

孔子说："我曾经整日不吃饭，整夜不睡觉，用来思考，结果没有获益，还不如学习为好呢。"

【英译】

The Master said, "For a period, I spent the whole time thinking without eating any food nor taking any sleep, but to no avail. It would have been better if I had spent the time learning."

15.31 子曰："吾尝终日不食，终夜不寝，以思，无益，不如学也。"

卫灵公第十五　Chapter Fifteen

孔子说："君子担心学不到道，而不担心贫穷。"

The Master said, "A man of virtue is concerned with the neglect of morality and justice, not hardship or poverty."

15.32
zǐ yuē　　　jūn zǐ móu dào bù móu shí　gēng yě　　něi zài qí zhōng
子曰："君子谋道不谋食。耕也，馁在其中
yǐ　　xué yě　　lù zài qí zhōng yǐ　　jūn zǐ yōu dào bù yōu pín
矣；学也，禄在其中矣。君子忧道不忧贫。"

【释义】

孔子说："君子只谋求道德，不谋求衣食。耕田，也常要饿肚子；学习，却能做官得到俸禄。所以君子担心学不到道，而不担心贫穷。"

【英译】

The Master said, "A man of virtue pursues morality and justice instead of means of living. Even if a man manually farms, he may still suffer from hunger; but if a man studies hard, he can secure a position and get a salary. A man of virtue is concerned with the neglect of morality and justice, not hardship or poverty."

Chapter Fifteen 卫灵公第十五

孔子说:"智慧足以得到它,仁德不能守住它,即使得到了它,必定会失掉它。"

The Master said, "For a thing that one has attained through wisdom, if it can not be retained by virtue, then even if it is attained, it is bound to be lost."

15.33

zǐ yuē　　　zhì jí zhī　　rén bù néng shǒu zhī　suī dé zhī　　bì shī
子曰:"知及之,仁不能守之,虽得之,必失
zhī　　zhì jí zhī　　rén néng shǒu zhī　　bù zhuāng yǐ lì zhī　zé mín
之。知及之,仁能守之,不庄以莅之,则民
bú jìng　　zhì jí zhī　　rén néng shǒu zhī　　zhuāng yǐ lì zhī　dòng zhī bù
不敬。知及之,仁能守之,庄以莅之,动之不
yǐ lǐ　　wèi shàn yě
以礼,未善也。"

【释义】

孔子说:"智慧足以得到它,仁德不能守住它,即使得到了它,必定会失掉它。智慧足以得到它,仁德能够守住它,却不用端庄的仪态来治理它,那么老百姓就不尊敬你。智慧足以得到它,仁德能够守住它,能用端庄的仪态来治理它,却不按礼来行动,那还没有达到至善的地步。"

【英译】

The Master said, "For a thing that one has attained through wisdom, if it can not be retained by virtue, then even if it is attained, it is bound to be lost; for a thing one has attained through wisdom and retained by virtue, if it is not governed with dignity, then it can not win your common people's respect; for a thing one has attained through wisdom, retained by virtue and governed by dignity, if it is not put to use in accord with etiquette, then it is less than perfect."

卫灵公第十五　Chapter Fifteen

【释义】

孔子说:"君子不可以做小事情而可以承担重任,小人不可以承担重任而可以做小事情。"

【英译】

The Master said, "A man of virtue can be entrusted with big missions, but should not be bothered with small things. A petty-minded man should not be entrusted with big missions, but can be assigned small tasks."

孔子说:"君子不可以做小事情而可以承担重任,小人不可以承担重任而可以做小事情。"

The Master said, "A man of virtue can be entrusted with big missions, but should not be bothered with small things. A petty-minded man should not be entrusted with big missions, but can be assigned small tasks."

15.34
zǐ yuē　　jūn zǐ bù kě xiǎo zhī ér kě dà shòu yě　xiǎo rén bù kě
子曰:"君子不可小知而可大受也,小人不可
dà shòu ér kě xiǎo zhī yě
大受而可小知也。"

Chapter Fifteen　卫灵公第十五

孔子说："老百姓对于仁的需要，超过了对水火的需要。我只见过人跳到水火中而死的，没有见过实行仁德而死的。"

The Master said, "The common people's thirst for virtue surpasses their need for water and fire. I have only seen people who die by jumping into water or fire, but I have not seen anyone die by following the course of virtue."

15.35
zǐ yuē　　　mín zhī yú rén yě　　shèn yú shuǐ huǒ　　shuǐ huǒ　　wú jiàn
子曰："民之于仁也，甚于水火。水火，吾见
dǎo ér sǐ zhě yǐ　　wèi jiàn dǎo rén ér sǐ zhě yě
蹈而死者矣，未见蹈仁而死者也。"

【释义】

孔子说："老百姓对于仁的需要，超过了对水火的需要。我只见过人跳到水火中而死的，没有见过实行仁德而死的。"

【英译】

The Master said, "The common people's thirst for virtue surpasses their need for water and fire. I have only seen people who die by jumping into water or fire, but I have not seen anyone die by following the course of virtue."

卫灵公第十五　Chapter Fifteen

【释义】

孔子说:"面临实践仁道的时机,连老师也不谦让。"

【英译】

The Master said, "In practicing virtue, do not hesitate to outperform your teacher."

孔子说:"面临实践仁道的时机,连老师也不谦让。"

The Master said, "In practicing virtue, do not hesitate to outperform your teacher."

15.36
zǐ yuē　　dāng rén　　bú ràng yú shī
子曰:"当仁,不让于师。"

Chapter Fifteen 卫灵公第十五

孔子说："君子诚信，但不拘于小信。"

The Master said, "A man of virtue values integrity, but is not rigid in trivial things."

【释义】

孔子说："君子诚信，但不拘于小信。"

【英译】

The Master said, "A man of virtue values integrity, but is not rigid in trivial things."

15.37
zǐ yuē　　　jūn zǐ zhēn ér bú liàng
子曰："君子贞而不谅。"

卫灵公第十五　Chapter Fifteen

孔子说："侍奉君主，应该认真地对待自己的职事，而把俸禄放到后面。"

The Master said, "In serving a ruler, give priority to the fulfillment of your duty. Consideration of salary should come after that."

【释义】

孔子说："侍奉君主，应该认真地对待自己的职事，而把俸禄放到后面。"

【英译】

The Master said, "In serving a ruler, give priority to the fulfillment of your duty. Consideration of salary should come after that."

15.38
zǐ yuē　　shì jūn　　jìng qí shì ér hòu qí shí
子曰："事君，敬其事而后其食。"

Chapter Fifteen　卫灵公第十五

孔子说："对任何人都可以有所教诲，没有种类的限制。"

The Master said, "Education should be accessible to everyone, regardless of their background."

【释义】

孔子说："对任何人都可以有所教诲，没有种类的限制。"

【英译】

The Master said, "Education should be accessible to everyone, regardless of their background."

15.39
zǐ yuē　　yǒu jiào wú lèi
子曰："有教无类。"

卫灵公第十五　Chapter Fifteen

孔子说："各人主张的道不同，决不共相谋事。"

The Master said, "For people who follow different courses, there is no point in consulting one another."

【释义】

孔子说："各人主张的道不同，决不共相谋事。"

【英译】

The Master said, "For people who follow different courses, there is no point in consulting one another."

15.40
zǐ yuē　　dào bù tóng　　bù xiāng wéi móu
子曰："道不同，不相为谋。"

Chapter Fifteen　卫灵公第十五

孔子说："言辞能够表情达意就可以了。"

The Master said, "In terms of words, as long as they convey the message, they are fine."

【释义】

孔子说："言辞能够表情达意就可以了。"

【英译】

The Master said, "In terms of words, as long as they convey the message, they are fine."

15.41
zǐ yuē　　　cí dá ér yǐ yǐ
子曰："辞达而已矣。"

卫灵公第十五　Chapter Fifteen

子张问道："这是同盲乐师讲话的礼道吗？"孔子说："是的，这本来就是帮助盲乐师的礼道。"

Zi Zhang asked, "Was that the way to receive a blind musician?" The Master answered, "Yes, that was my way to help a blind musician."

15.42

shī miǎn jiàn　　jí jiē　　zǐ yuē　　jiē yě　　jí xí　　zǐ yuē
师　冕　见，及 阶，子 曰："阶 也。"及 席，子 曰：
　　xí yě　　　jiē zuò　　zǐ gào zhī yuē　　mǒu zài sī　　mǒu zài
"席 也。"皆 坐，子 告 之 曰："某 在 斯，某 在
sī
斯。"
shī miǎn chū　　zǐ zhāng wèn yuē　　yǔ shī yán zhī dào yú　　zǐ yuē
师 冕 出。子 张 问 曰："与 师 言 之 道 与？"子 曰：
　rán　　gù xiàng shī zhī dào yě
"然，固 相 师 之 道 也。"

【释义】

师冕来见孔子，走到台阶前，孔子便说："这是台阶。"走到坐席前，孔子便说："这是坐席。"都坐定之后，孔子便告诉他说："某人在这里，某人在这里。"

师冕告辞离开了。子张问道："这是同盲乐师讲话的礼道吗？"孔子说："是的，这本来就是帮助盲乐师的礼道。"

【英译】

Shi Mian, a blind musician came to visit the Master. When he approached the steps, the Master said, "Here are the steps." When he came near the mat, the Master said, "Here is the mat." After they sat down, the Master introduced to him, "So and so is sitting here, and so and so is sitting there."

After the musician left, Zi Zhang asked, "Was that the way to receive a blind musician?" The Master answered, "Yes, that was my way to help a blind musician."

jì shì dì shí liù
季氏第十六
CHAPTER SIXTEEN

季氏第十六　Chapter Sixteen

孔子说："季孙的忧患不在颛臾，而在鲁国的宫墙之内啊！"

The Master said, "What Ji should be concerned with is not Zhuanyu, but the chaos within the court."

【释义】

　　季氏将要攻打颛臾。冉有、季路拜见孔子说："季氏将要对颛臾采取军事行动。"

　　孔子说："求！这难道不该责备你们吗？颛臾，当初先王让它做东蒙山的主祭，而且它又是在鲁国国境之内，这是鲁国的重要臣属啊，为什么要攻打它呢？"

　　冉有说："季氏想要这样做，我们两个都不想这样做。"

【英译】

　　The head of the Ji family was about to launch an attack on Zhuanyu. Ran You (Ran Qiu) and Ji Lu, who were serving as stewards for the Ji family, went to see Confucius and said, "Our master is going to launch an attack on Zhuanyu."

　　The Master said, "Qiu! Shouldn't you be blamed for this? As for Zhuanyu, a former sovereign of ours had granted its ruler the right to preside over sacrifices to the East Meng Mountain. Besides, Zhuanyu is within the territory of the Lu State, and its ruler is subject to the Duke of Lu, why should it be attacked?"

　　Ran You answered, "It is our master who is determined to do so. Neither of us favors it."

16.1

jì shì jiāng fá zhuān yú　　rǎn yǒu　jì lù jiàn yú kǒng zǐ yuē　　jì
季氏将伐颛臾。冉有、季路见于孔子曰："季
shì jiāng yǒu shì yú zhuān yú
氏将有事于颛臾。"

kǒng zǐ yuē　　qiú　wú nǎi ěr shì guò yú　　fú zhuān yú　　xī zhě
孔子曰："求！无乃尔是过与？夫颛臾，昔者
xiān wáng yǐ wéi dōng méng zhǔ　　qiě zài bāng yù zhī zhōng yǐ　　shì shè jì
先王以为东蒙主，且在邦域之中矣，是社稷
zhī chén yě　　hé yǐ fá wéi
之臣也，何以伐为？"

rǎn yǒu yuē　　fū zǐ yù zhī　　wú èr chén zhě jiē bú yù yě
冉有曰："夫子欲之，吾二臣者皆不欲也。"

Chapter Sixteen 季氏第十六

孔子曰:"求!周任有言曰:'陈力就列,不能者止。'危而不持,颠而不扶,则将焉用彼相矣?且尔言过矣。虎兕出于柙,龟玉毁于椟中,是谁之过与?"

冉有曰:"今夫颛臾,固而近于费。今不取,后世必为子孙忧。"

【释义】

孔子说:"求!周任有句话说:'能施展才能的,就接受这个职务;不能施展才能的,就应辞职。'如果盲人站不稳而不能去扶持他,摔倒了又不能把他扶起来,那么又用那个护理人干什么呢?而且,你的话显然说错了。老虎、犀牛从笼子里跑出来,龟甲、美玉在匣中被毁坏,这是谁的过错呢?"

冉有说:"颛臾现在城墙坚固而且靠近季氏的采邑费城。现在如果不去占领它,将来必定会成为子孙的忧患。"

【英译】

The Master said, "Qiu! The famous ancient official Zhou Ren said this, 'When one can serve and fulfill his duty, one takes office; otherwise, he quits.' If you don't render protection when your master is in danger, or don't give him a helping hand when he is about to fall, what are you good for? Moreover, what you said just now is wrong. If a tiger or a rhinoceros broke loose from its cage, or tortoise shells and fine jade are damaged in their caskets, whose fault is it?"

Ran You said, "Zhuanyu is strongly fortified and is close to Bi. If it is not taken now, I'm afraid it will become a source of trouble for later generations."

季氏第十六 Chapter Sixteen

孔子曰："求！君子疾夫舍曰'欲之'而必为之辞。丘也闻有国有家者，不患寡而患不均，不患贫而患不安。盖均无贫，和无寡，安无倾。"

【释义】

孔子说："求！君子最痛恨那种嘴上不说'想要得到它'而一定要替自己的行为找借口的人。我听说，不管是有封地的诸侯还是有食邑的大臣，不担心财产少，只担心财富分配不均；不担心人口少，只担心国家不安定。因为财富平均，就无所谓贫穷；上下和睦，就不觉得人口少；境内安定，国家就不会倾覆。"

【英译】

The Master said, "Qiu! A man of virtue detests those who use farfetched excuses to try to justify their greed. I have heard that for the ruler of a state or a noble family, what he is concerned with most is not poverty, but rather the uneven distribution of wealth; not the lack of people, but unrest and insurgency. Where even distribution is achieved, poverty doesn't pose a problem; where harmony is achieved, lack of people doesn't pose a problem; and where stability is achieved, a state is in no danger of being overthrown."

Chapter Sixteen 季氏第十六

"夫如是，故远人不服，则修文德以来之。既来之，则安之。今由与求也，相夫子，远人不服而不能来也；邦分崩离析而不能守也，而谋动干戈于邦内。吾恐季孙之忧不在颛臾，而在萧墙之内也。"

【释义】

"正因为这样做了，所以远方的人如果不归顺，就应该加强文教德化来使他们归顺。他们归顺之后，就要使他们安顿下来。现在你们两个人辅佐季氏，远方的人不归顺却不能使他们来投奔；国家四分五裂，你们却不能保全，反而策划在国境内发动战争。我担心季孙的忧患不在颛臾，而在鲁国的宫墙之内啊！"

【英译】

"When all the above are achieved, if people from distant places still do not submit themselves, then promote etiquette and music and try to attract them with the practice of virtue. After they come for submission, help them settle down. Now Zi Lu and Ran You, as aides to the head of the Ji family, you fail to do anything when the distant people are not attracted; nor can you do anything to the state when it is about to disintegrate. What's worse, you are plotting on a war within our state. I believe what Ji should be concerned with is not Zhuanyu, but the chaos within the court."

季氏第十六 Chapter Sixteen

孔子说:"天下清明,那么制礼作乐和发令征伐的权力都出自天子;天下昏乱,那么制礼作乐和发令征伐的权力都出自诸侯。"

The Master said, "When the Way prevails in the world, it is the sovereign who has the final say on such issues as rituals, music and punitive expeditions. When the Way does not prevail, then it is the dukes who have the final say on such issues."

16.2

kǒng zǐ yuē tiān xià yǒu dào zé lǐ yuè zhēng fá zì tiān zǐ chū
孔子曰:"天下有道,则礼乐征伐自天子出;
tiān xià wú dào zé lǐ yuè zhēng fá zì zhū hóu chū zì zhū hóu chū
天下无道,则礼乐征伐自诸侯出。自诸侯出,
gài shí shì xī bù shī yǐ zì dà fū chū wǔ shì xī bù shī yǐ
盖十世希不失矣;自大夫出,五世希不失矣;
péi chén zhí guó mìng sān shì xī bù shī yǐ tiān xià yǒu dào zé zhèng
陪臣执国命,三世希不失矣。天下有道,则政
bú zài dà fū tiān xià yǒu dào zé shù rén bú yì
不在大夫。天下有道,则庶人不议。"

【释义】

孔子说:"天下清明,那么制礼作乐和发令征伐的权力都出自天子;天下昏乱,那么制礼作乐和发令征伐的权力都出自诸侯。出自诸侯,大约传至十代很少有不失掉的;出自大夫,传至五代很少有不失掉的;如果是家臣操纵了国家政令,传至三代很少有不失掉的。天下清明,那么政令不会出大夫。天下清明,那么老百姓就不非议政治了。"

【英译】

The Master said, "When the Way prevails in the world, it is the sovereign who has the final say on such issues as rituals, music and punitive expeditions. When the Way does not prevail, then it is the dukes who have the final say on such issues. If the decision-making power lies with the dukes, then the empire will most probably last no more than ten generations; if the power falls into the hands of the senior officials, then the empire will most probably last no more than five generations; if the power lies with still lower ranking officials, then the empire will most probably last no more than three generations. When the Way prevails, the power will not lie with senior officials, and the common people will not speak ill of the government."

Chapter Sixteen 季氏第十六

孔子说："鲁国的权力从鲁君手中失掉已经五代了，政权落到大夫手里已经四代了，因此鲁国三家的子孙已经衰微了。"

The Master said, "It has been five generations since the Duke of the Lu State lost his power. It has been four generations since the power fell into the hands of the senior officials. Consequently, the descendants of the duke have been on the decline."

16.3
kǒng zǐ yuē　　　lù zhī qù gōng shì wǔ shì yǐ　　zhèng dài yú dà fū
孔子曰："禄之去公室五世矣，政逮于大夫
sì shì yǐ　　gù fú sān huán zhī zǐ sūn wēi yǐ
四世矣，故夫三桓之子孙微矣。"

【释义】

孔子说："鲁国的权力从鲁君手中失掉已经五代了，政权落到大夫手里已经四代了，因此鲁国三家的子孙已经衰微了。"

【英译】

The Master said, "It has been five generations since the Duke of the Lu State lost his power. It has been four generations since the power fell into the hands of the senior officials. Consequently, the descendants of the duke have been on the decline."

季氏第十六　Chapter Sixteen

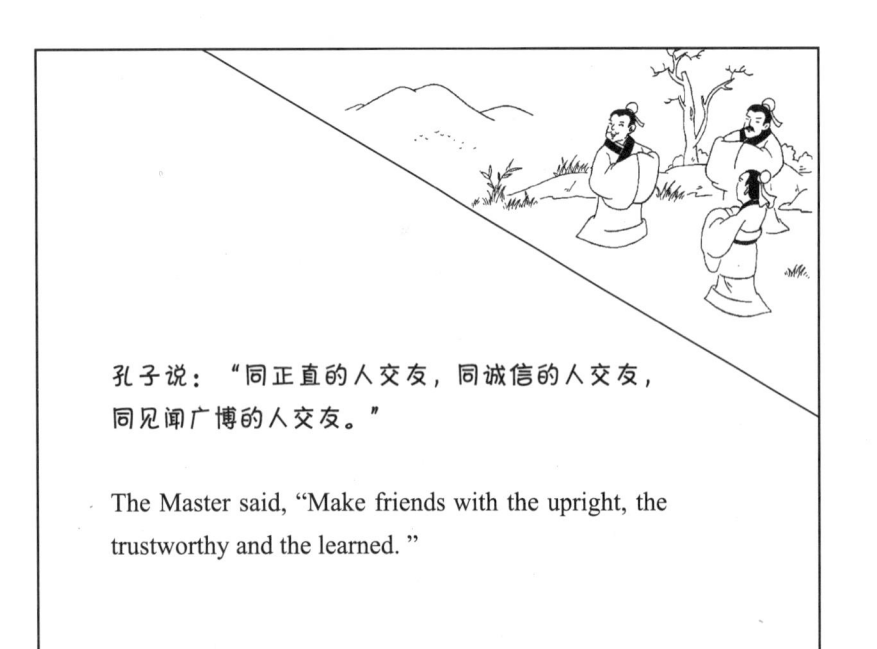

孔子说："同正直的人交友，同诚信的人交友，同见闻广博的人交友。"

The Master said, "Make friends with the upright, the trustworthy and the learned."

16.4
孔子曰："益者三友，损者三友。友直，友谅，友多闻，益矣。友便辟，友善柔，友便佞，损矣。"

kǒng zǐ yuē　yì zhě sān yǒu　sǔn zhě sān yǒu　yǒu zhí　yǒu liàng　yǒu duō wén　yì yǐ　yǒu pián pì　yǒu shàn róu　yǒu pián nìng　sǔn yǐ

【释义】

孔子说："有益的交友情况有三种，有害的交友情况有三种。同正直的人交友，同诚信的人交友，同见闻广博的人交友，便有益了。同逢迎谄媚的人交友，同善于装出和颜悦色骗人的人交友，同惯于花言巧语的人交友，便有害了。"

【英译】

The Master said, "Friendship with the three kinds of people will do you good, namely friendship with the upright, the trustworthy and the learned. In contrast, friendship with another three kinds of people will do you harm, namely friendship with the hypocritical, the double-faced and the smooth-tongued."

Chapter Sixteen 季氏第十六

孔子说："以礼乐调节自己为乐，以称道别人的好处为乐，以有许多贤人做朋友为乐。"

The Master said, "Enjoy yourself in conforming to etiquette and music in both words and action, enjoy yourself in discussing other people's merits, and enjoy yourself in making friends with the virtuous and the capable."

16.5

kǒng zǐ yuē　　yì zhě sān lè　　sǔn zhě sān lè　　lè jié lǐ yuè
孔子曰："益者三乐，损者三乐。乐节礼乐，
lè dào rén zhī shàn　　lè duō xián yǒu　　yì yǐ　　lè jiāo lè　　lè yì
乐道人之善，乐多贤友，益矣。乐骄乐，乐佚
yóu　　lè yàn lè　　sǔn yǐ
游，乐宴乐，损矣。"

【释义】

孔子说："有益的快乐有三种，有害的快乐有三种。以礼乐调节自己为乐，以称道别人的好处为乐，以有许多贤人做朋友为乐，便有益了。喜欢骄纵无节制地作乐，喜欢游荡忘返，喜欢沉溺于饮酒作乐，便有害了。"

【英译】

The Master said, "Enjoyment in three kinds of things will do you good, namely enjoyment in conforming to etiquette and music in both words and action, enjoyment in discussing other people's merits, and enjoyment in making friends with the virtuous and the capable. In contrast, enjoyment in three other things will do you harm, namely enjoyment in arrogance and self-indulgence, enjoyment in wildness in words and behavior, and enjoyment in addiction to partying and banqueting."

季氏第十六　Chapter Sixteen

孔子说："话未到该说的时候却说了，叫做急躁；话到了该说的时候却不说，叫做隐瞒。"

The Master said, "In one's relationship with a man of virtue, one is prone to make three kinds of mistakes: to say things that should not be said yet is being rash; to keep quiet on things that should be said is evasive."

16.6
kǒng zǐ yuē　　shì yú jūn zǐ yǒu sān qiān　yán wèi jí zhī ér yán
孔子曰："侍于君子有三愆：言未及之而言，
wèi zhī zào　　yán jí zhī ér bù yán　　wèi zhī yǐn　　wèi jiàn yán sè ér
谓之躁；言及之而不言，谓之隐；未见颜色而
yán　wèi zhī gǔ
言，谓之瞽。"

【释义】

孔子说："侍奉君子往往有三种过失：话未到该说的时候却说了，叫做急躁；话到了该说的时候却不说，叫做隐瞒；未曾察颜观色却贸然开口，叫做瞎眼。"

【英译】

The Master said, "In one's relationship with a man of virtue, one is prone to make three kinds of mistakes: to say things that should not be said yet is being rash; to keep quiet on things that should be said is evasive; to blurt without paying attention to the listener's facial expressions is being blind."

Chapter Sixteen　季氏第十六

【释义】

孔子说："君子有三种戒忌：年少的时候，血气还未发育定，应该戒忌的在于女色；到了壮年之时，血气正旺盛刚烈，应该戒忌的在于争斗；到了老年之时，血气已经衰退，应该戒忌的在于贪得无厌。"

【英译】

The Master said, "A man of virtue should guard against three things. In youth, when the blood and energy have not completely settled, he should guard against lust; in the prime of life, when the blood and energy are exuberant, he should guard against contentions; in old age, when the blood and energy are on the wane, he should guard against greed."

16.7

kǒng zǐ yuē　　jūn zǐ yǒu sān jiè　　shào zhī shí　　xuè qì wèi dìng
孔子曰："君子有三戒：少之时，血气未定，
jiè zhī zài sè　　jí qí zhuàng yě　　xuè qì fāng gāng　　jiè zhī zài dòu
戒之在色；及其壮也，血气方刚，戒之在斗；
jí qí lǎo yě　　xuè qì jì shuāi　　jiè zhī zài dé
及其老也，血气既衰，戒之在得。"

季氏第十六　Chapter Sixteen

孔子说："君子敬畏三件事：敬畏天命，敬畏地位高贵的人，敬畏圣人的话。"

The Master said, "For a man of virtue, there are three things he holds in awe: the Mandate of Heaven, people in high positions, and words from sages."

16.8
kǒng zǐ yuē　　　jūn zǐ yǒu sān wèi　　wèi tiān mìng　　wèi dà rén　　wèi
孔子曰："君子有三畏：畏天命，畏大人，畏
shèng rén zhī yán　xiǎo rén bù zhī tiān mìng ér bú wèi yě　　xiá dà rén
圣人之言。小人不知天命而不畏也，狎大人，
wǔ shèng rén zhī yán
侮圣人之言。"

【释义】

孔子说："君子敬畏三件事：敬畏天命，敬畏地位高贵的人，敬畏圣人的话。小人不懂天命，因而也不敬畏，不尊重地位高贵的人，轻侮圣人的话。"

【英译】

The Master said, "For a man of virtue, there are three things he holds in awe: the Mandate of Heaven, people in high positions, and words from sages. For a petty-minded man, he doesn't hold the Mandate of Heaven in awe due to his ignorance of its divinity. Moreover, he treats people in high positions disrespectfully and slights the words of sages."

Chapter Sixteen 季氏第十六

孔子说:"生下来就知道的,是上等;经过学习才知道的,是次一等;遇到困惑才学习的,又次一等;遇到困惑仍不学习,这样的人就是下等了。"

The Master said, "Those who are born with wisdom belong to the top class; those who acquire wisdom through learning come second; those who learn only when confronted with confusion come next; those who refuse to learn even when confronted with confusion come last."

16.9

kǒng zǐ yuē shēng ér zhī zhī zhě shàng yě xué ér zhī zhī zhě
孔子曰:"生而知之者,上也;学而知之者,
cì yě kùn ér xué zhī yòu qí cì yě kùn ér bù xué mín sī
次也;困而学之,又其次也;困而不学,民斯
wéi xià yǐ
为下矣。"

【释义】

孔子说:"生下来就知道的,是上等;经过学习才知道的,是次一等;遇到困惑才学习的,又次一等;遇到困惑仍不学习,这样的人就是下等了。"

【英译】

The Master said, "Those who are born with wisdom belong to the top class; those who acquire wisdom through learning come second; those who learn only when confronted with confusion come next; those who refuse to learn even when confronted with confusion come last."

季氏第十六　Chapter Sixteen

孔子说："办事，要考虑是不是谨慎严肃；看见可以有所得，要考虑是否合于义的要求。"

The Master said, "Be deferential and prudent in conduct, and in the face of gain, think about whether one deserves it."

16.10
孔子曰："君子有九思：视思明，听思聪，色思温，貌思恭，言思忠，事思敬，疑思问，忿思难，见得思义。"

【释义】

孔子说："君子有九种要考虑的事：看的时候，要考虑是不是看明白了；听的时候，要考虑是不是听清楚了；自己的脸色，要考虑是不是温和；容貌态度，要考虑是不是谦恭；言语说话，要考虑是不是忠诚；办事，要考虑是不是谨慎严肃；遇到疑问，要考虑向人家请教；忿怒时，要考虑是不是会有后患；看见可以有所得，要考虑是否合于义的要求。"

【英译】

The Master said, "A man of virtue thinks about the following nine things: in using his eye, does he get a clear vision? In using his ears, does he hear clearly? In terms of his facial expression, does he look amiable? About his attitude, is he respectful? When speaking to others, are his words trustworthy? As for his conduct, is he deferential and prudent? When he has questions, does he seek answers by asking other people? When in anger, does he consider the consequences? In the face of gain, does he think about whether he deserves it?"

Chapter Sixteen 季氏第十六

孔子说:"看到善良的行为,就担心自身做不到;看到不善良的行为,就好像把手伸到开水中一样赶快避开。"

The Master said, "Be eager to pursue goodness as if you can't wait, and be eager to evade evil in the same way you evade boiling water."

16.11
kǒng zǐ yuē　　jiàn shàn rú bù jí　　jiàn bú shàn rú tàn tāng　　wú jiàn
孔子曰:"见善如不及,见不善如探汤。吾见
qí rén yǐ　　wú wén qí yǔ yǐ　　yǐn jū yǐ qiú qí zhì　　xíng yì yǐ
其人矣,吾闻其语矣。隐居以求其志,行义以
dá qí dào　　wú wén qí yǔ yǐ　　wèi jiàn qí rén yě
达其道。吾闻其语矣,未见其人也。"

【释义】

孔子说:"看到善良的行为,就担心自身做不到;看到不善的行为,就好像把手伸到开水中一样赶快避开。我见到过这样的人,也听到过这样的话。以隐居避世来保全自己的志向,依照义而贯彻自己的主张。我听到过这样的话,却没有见到过这样的人。"

【英译】

The Master said, "Be eager to pursue goodness as if you can't wait, and be eager to evade evil in the same way you evade boiling water. I have seen such people and I have heard such words. Live in seclusion so as to keep one's aspiration, and achieve one's political goal by conforming to ethics and justice. I have heard such words, but have never seen such people."

季氏第十六　Chapter Sixteen

伯夷、叔齐饿死在首阳山下，老百姓直到现在还称赞他们。

Bo Yi and Shu Qi had starved to death at the foot of the Shouyang Hill, yet even today the common people still sing their praises.

16.12 齐景公有马千驷，死之日，民无德而称焉。伯夷、叔齐饿于首阳之下，民到于今称之。其斯之谓与？

【释义】

齐景公纵然有四千匹马，死的时候，百姓没有因感激而赞赏他的。伯夷、叔齐饿死在首阳山下，老百姓直到现在还称赞他们。大概就是说的这个吧？

【英译】

Duke Jing of the Qi State had possessed four thousand horses, yet when he died, he received no compliments from any of the common people. In contrast, Bo Yi and Shu Qi had starved to death at the foot of the Shouyang Hill, yet even today the common people still sing their praises. I guess these can be regarded as evidence of what we have just discussed.

Chapter Sixteen　季氏第十六

孔子说："不学《诗》，就不懂得怎样说话；不学礼，就不懂得怎样立身。"

The Master said, "Without knowledge from *The Book of Songs*, you can't speak properly; without knowing the proper etiquette, you can't conduct yourself properly."

16.13
chén gāng wèn yú bó yú yuē　　　　zǐ yì yǒu yì wén hū
陈　亢　问　于　伯　鱼　曰："子　亦　有　异　闻　乎？"
duì yuē　　wèi yě　cháng dú lì　　lǐ qū ér guò tíng　 yuē　xué
对　曰："未　也。尝　独　立，鲤　趋　而　过　庭。曰：'学
shī hū　　　duì yuē　　wèi yě　　　　bù xué shī　wú
《诗》乎？'对　曰：'未　也。' '不　学《诗》，无
yǐ yán　　　lǐ tuì ér xué shī
以　言。'鲤　退　而　学《诗》。"

【释义】

陈亢问孔子的儿子伯鱼说："你在你父亲那里听到过特别的教导吗？"

伯鱼回答说："没有。有一次他独自站在堂上，我恭敬地快步从庭中走过。他说：'学《诗》了没有？'我回答说：'没有。'他说：'不学《诗》，就不懂得怎样说话。'我退下去就学习《诗》。"

【英译】

Chen Gang asked Confucius' son Bo Yu, "Have you learned extraordinary things from the Master?"

Bo Yu answered, "No. One time Father was standing alone in the courtyard. As I was passing by respectfully with quick steps, he asked me, 'Have you studied *The Book of Songs*?' I said no. He then said, 'Without knowledge from *The Book of Songs*, you can't speak properly.' I retreated and started to learn *The Book of Songs*."

季氏第十六　Chapter Sixteen

"他日，又独立，鲤趋而过庭。曰：'学礼乎？'对曰：'未也。''不学礼，无以立。'鲤退而学礼。闻斯二者。"

陈亢退而喜曰："问一得三：闻《诗》，闻礼，又闻君子之远其子也。"

【释义】

"又有一天，他又独自站在堂上，我恭敬地快步走过庭院。他说：'学礼了没有？'我回答说：'没有。'他说：'不学礼，就不懂得怎样立身。'我回去就学习礼。我就听到这两次。"

陈亢回去高兴地说："我问一件事，得到了三点收获：听到了关于《诗》的道理，听到了关于礼的道理，还得知君子不偏爱自己的儿子。"

【英译】

Another day Father was again standing alone in the courtyard. And again as I was passing by respectfully with quick steps, he asked, 'Have you studied etiquette?' I answered no. He then said, 'Without knowing the proper etiquette, you can't conduct yourself properly.' So I retreated and started to study etiquette. These are the two things I have learned from Father."

Chen Gang retreated and said happily, "I asked about one thing and yet got the answers to three. I have learned about the importance of *The Book of Songs* and the etiquette, and I have also learned that a man of virtue doesn't have partiality for his own son."

Chapter Sixteen 季氏第十六

国君的妻子，国君称她为夫人，夫人自称为小童。

The wife of a sovereign was called "my lady" by the sovereign, "this humble youth" by herself.

16.14
bāng jūn zhī qī, jūn chēng zhī yuē fū rén, fū rén zì chēng yuē xiǎo tóng;
邦君之妻，君称之曰夫人，夫人自称曰小童；
bāng rén chēng zhī yuē jūn fū rén, chēng zhū yì bāng yuē guǎ xiǎo jūn; yì
邦人称之曰君夫人，称诸异邦曰寡小君；异
bāng rén chēng zhī yì yuē jūn fū rén
邦人称之亦曰君夫人。

【释义】

国君的妻子，国君称她为夫人，夫人自称为小童；本国人称她为君夫人，对外国人称她为寡小君；外国人称她也叫君夫人。

【英译】

The wife of a sovereign was called "my lady" by the sovereign, "this humble youth" by herself and "the lady of the lord" by the people in same the country. In the presence of people from other countries, the sovereign called her "my little lord", and the foreigners called her "lady of the lord".

阳货第十七

CHAPTER SEVENTEEN

Chapter Seventeen 阳货第十七

阳货想见孔子，孔子不见他，于是便赠送孔子一只小猪。孔子等他不在家的时候，前往拜谢以还礼。不巧在路上遇见阳货。

Yang Huo, a steward of the Ji family, wanted to see the Master, but the Master rejected his request. Yang Huo then sent the Master a piglet as a gift. The Master purposefully chose a time when Yang Huo was not home and went to pay him a courtesy visit. However, the two of them met each other on the way.

17.1

yáng huò yù jiàn kǒng zǐ　　kǒng zǐ bú jiàn　　kuì kǒng zǐ tún　　kǒng zǐ sì
阳货欲见孔子，孔子不见，归孔子豚。孔子时
qí wáng yě　　ér wǎng bài zhī　　yù zhū tú
其亡也，而往拜之。遇诸涂。
wèi kǒng zǐ yuē　　lái　　yú yǔ ěr yán　　yuē　　huái qí bǎo
谓孔子曰："来！予与尔言。"曰："怀其宝
ér mí qí bāng　　kě wèi rén hū　　yuē　　bù kě
而迷其邦，可谓仁乎？"曰："不可。"

【释义】

阳货想见孔子，孔子不见他，于是便赠送孔子一只小猪。孔子等他不在家的时候，前往拜谢以还礼。不巧在路上遇见阳货。

阳货对孔子说："过来！我跟你讲话。"于是说："把自己的本领藏起来，任凭自己的国家混乱不已，能够说是仁吗？"孔子说："不能说是仁。"

【英译】

Yang Huo, a steward of the Ji family, wanted to see the Master, but the Master rejected his request. Yang Huo then sent the Master a piglet as a gift. The Master purposefully chose a time when Yang Huo was not home and went to pay him a courtesy visit. However, the two of them met each other on the way.

Yang Huo said, "Come! I want to talk to you." He then asked, "Can we call him a virtuous man who hides his capabilities to allow his country to suffer chaos?" The Master said, "No."

205

"好从事而亟失时，可谓知乎？"曰："不可。""日月逝矣，岁不我与。"孔子曰："诺，吾将仕矣。"

【释义】

阳货又说："自己喜欢从政却又屡次错失时机，能够说是智吗？"孔子说："不能说是智。"阳货又说："时间流逝，岁月不等我们啊。"孔子说："好吧，我就要做官了。"

【英译】

Yang Huo then asked, "Can we call him a wise man who is interested in governance and yet repeatedly failed to grasp the opportunities?" The Master said, "No." Yang Huo then said, "Time flies and it doesn't wait for any of us." The Master said with reluctance, "Fine, I will hold an official position."

Chapter Seventeen　阳货第十七

孔子说："人的本性是相近的，由于习性不同才相差很远。"

The Master said, "People are born alike in nature, but their customs and practices are very different."

【释义】

孔子说："人的本性是相近的，由于习性不同才相差很远。"

【英译】

The Master said, "People are born alike in nature, but their customs and practices are very different."

17.2

zǐ yuē　　xìng xiāng jìn yě　　xí xiāng yuǎn yě
子曰："性相近也，习相远也。"

阳货第十七　Chapter Seventeen

孔子说："只有上等的智者与下等的愚人是不会改变的。"

The Master said, "Only the wise of the top class and the stupid of the lowest class refuse to change."

17.3
zǐ yuē　　　wéi shàng zhì yǔ xià yú bù yí
子曰："唯　上　知　与　下　愚　不　移。"

【释义】

　　孔子说："只有上等的智者与下等的愚人是不会改变的。"

【英译】

　　The Master said, "Only the wise of the top class and the stupid of the lowest class refuse to change."

Chapter Seventeen　阳货第十七

孔子说:"杀鸡何必用牛刀呢?"

The Master said, "Why use an ox-cleaver to kill a chicken?"

17.4
zǐ zhī wǔ chéng, wén xián gē zhī shēng。 fū zǐ wǎn ěr ér xiào yuē:
子之武城,闻弦歌之声。夫子莞尔而笑曰:
gē jī yān yòng niú dāo? zǐ yóu duì yuē: xī zhě yǎn yě wén
"割鸡焉用牛刀?"子游对曰:"昔者偃也闻
zhū fū zǐ yuē: jūn zǐ xué dào zé ài rén, xiǎo rén xué dào zé yì
诸夫子曰:'君子学道则爱人,小人学道则易
shǐ yě。 zǐ yuē: èr sān zǐ! yǎn zhī yán shì yě。 qián
使也。'"子曰:"二三子!偃之言是也。前
yán xì zhī ěr。
言戏之耳。"

【释义】

孔子到了武城,听到琴瑟歌诵的声音。孔子微微一笑,说:"杀鸡何必用牛刀呢?"邑宰子游回答说:"以前我听先生说过:'君子学礼乐之道就会爱人,小人学礼乐之道就容易使唤。'"孔子说:"弟子们!偃的话是对的。我刚才的话不过是跟他开玩笑罢了。"

【英译】

The Master went to Wucheng, where his student Zi You served as the magistrate. When he heard singing accompanied by stringed musical instrument, the Master smiled and said, "Why use an ox-cleaver to kill a chicken?" Zi You answered, "Earlier, I heard you say that 'When a man of virtue is taught music and etiquette, he will love people; and when a petty-minded is taught music and etiquette, he will become more obedient.'" Upon hearing this, the Master said to his disciples, "What Zi You just said is right. I was only joking just now."

209

阳货第十七　Chapter Seventeen

孔子说："如果有人能用我，我将在东方复兴周的世道！"

The Master said, "If I am offered a post, don't you think I can help restore the prosperity of the state?"

17.5
gōng shān fú rǎo yǐ bì pàn， zhào， zǐ yù wǎng。
公山弗扰以费畔，召，子欲往。
zǐ lù bú yuè， yuē： mò zhī yě yǐ， hé bì gōng shān shì zhī zhī yě？
子路不说，曰："末之也已，何必公山氏之之也？"
zǐ yuē： fú zhào wǒ zhě， ér qǐ tú zāi？ rú yǒu yòng wǒ zhě，wú qí wéi dōng zhōu hū！
子曰："夫召我者，而岂徒哉？如有用我者，吾其为东周乎！"

【释义】

公山弗扰在费邑准备反叛季氏，召孔子前去，孔子想去。

子路不高兴，说："没有地方去就算了，何必到公山弗扰那里呢？"

孔子说："那个召我去的人，难道就平白无故召我吗？如果有人能用我，我将在东方复兴周的世道！"

【英译】

Gongshan Furao, a steward of the Ji family, went to Bi and used it as a stronghold to launch an attack on the Ji family. He summoned the Master, who was inclined to go.

Zi Lu was displeased and said, "Is there nowhere else to go? Do you have to visit Gongshan Furao?"

The Master answered, "Don't you think he has a reason to summon me? If I am offered a post, don't you think I can help restore the prosperity of the state?"

Chapter Seventeen 阳货第十七

孔子说："要在天下实行恭敬、宽厚、信实、勤敏、慈惠五种品德。"

The Master said, "Deference, tolerance, trustworthiness, diligence, and generosity."

17.6
zǐ zhāng wèn rén yú kǒng zǐ。kǒng zǐ yuē： néng xíng wǔ zhě yú tiān
子张问仁于孔子。孔子曰："能行五者于天
xià， wéi rén yǐ
下，为仁矣。"
qǐng wèn zhī。 yuē： gōng kuān xìn mǐn huì。 gōng
"请问之。"曰："恭，宽，信，敏，惠。恭
zé bù wǔ， kuān zé dé zhòng， xìn zé rén rèn yān， mǐn zé yǒu gōng，
则不侮，宽则得众，信则人任焉，敏则有功，
huì zé zú yǐ shǐ rén
惠则足以使人。"

【释义】

子张向孔子问什么是仁。孔子说："能在天下实行五种品德，可以说就是仁了。"

子张说："请问是哪五种？"孔子说："恭敬，宽厚，信实，勤敏，慈惠。恭敬就不会受到侮辱，宽厚就能获得众人拥护，信实就会得到别人的信任，勤敏就会取得成功，慈惠就能够役使别人。"

【英译】

Zi Zhang asked about benevolence. The Master answered, "A man who can practice the five things everywhere under Heaven can be considered as having achieved benevolence."

Zi Zhang asked about the five things, and the Master answered, "Deference, tolerance, trustworthiness, diligence, and generosity. By being deferential, one does not incur insult; by being tolerant, one wins over the common people; by being trustworthy, one gains the trust and support of other people; by being diligent, one makes achievements; and by being generous, one can use the labor of other people."

孔子说："坚硬的东西，磨也磨不薄；洁白的东西，染也染不黑。"

The Master said, "What is really hard does not become thinner because of grinding, and what is pure can not be dyed black."

17.7

bì xī zhào, zǐ yù wǎng. zǐ lù yuē: xī zhě yóu yě wén zhū fū
佛肸召，子欲往。子路曰："昔者由也闻诸夫

zǐ yuē qīn yú qí shēn wéi bú shàn zhě jūn zǐ bú rù yě
子曰：'亲于其身为不善者，君子不入也。'

bì xī yǐ zhōng móu pàn zǐ zhī wǎng yě rú zhī hé zǐ yuē
佛肸以中牟畔，子之往也，如之何？"子曰：

rán yǒu shì yán yě bù yuē jiān hū mó ér bú lìn bù yuē bái
"然。有是言也。不曰坚乎，磨而不磷；不曰白

hū niè ér bù zī wú qǐ páo guā yě zāi yān néng xì ér bù shí
乎，涅而不缁。吾岂匏瓜也哉？焉能系而不食？"

【释义】

佛肸叫孔子前去，孔子想去。子路说："以前我听先生说过：'亲自做坏事的人那里，君子是不去的。'如今佛肸占据中牟造反，您却要去，这怎么说得过去呢？"孔子说："是的，我说过这样的话。但是，坚硬的东西，磨也磨不薄；洁白的东西，染也染不黑。我难道是个葫芦吗？怎么能只是挂在那里而不吃呢？"

【英译】

Bi Xi, the magistrate of Zhongmou, summoned the Master. The Master was inclined to go, but Zi Lu said in protest, "Earlier I have heard you say that 'A man of virtue would not visit a man who does evil.' Bi Xi used Zhongmou as a stronghold to rebel, and yet you are going to pay him a visit. How do you explain this?" The Master said, "Yes, I did say such things, but there is another saying: what is really hard does not become thinner because of grinding, and what is pure can not be dyed black. Am I a gourd that is not good enough for eating but is only good for decoration?"

Chapter Seventeen　阳货第十七

孔子说："爱好仁而不爱好学习，其弊病是容易受人愚弄；爱好智而不爱好学习，其弊病是好高骛远而没有基础。"

The Master said, "To love humaneness but not learning, one may easily be deceived; to love wisdom but not learning, one may aim too high yet without any foundation."

17.8

zǐ yuē　　　　yóu yě　　　　rǔ wén liù yán liù bì yǐ hū　　　　duì yuē
子曰："由也，女闻六言六蔽矣乎？"对曰：
wèi yě　　　　jū wú yù rǔ　　hào rén bú hào xué　　qí bì
"未也。""居！吾语女。好仁不好学，其蔽
yě yú　　hào zhì bú hào xué　　qí bì yě dàng　　hào xìn bú hào xué
也愚；好知不好学，其蔽也荡；好信不好学，
qí bì yě zéi　　hào zhí bú hào xué　　qí bì yě jiǎo　　hào yǒng bú hào
其蔽也贼；好直不好学，其蔽也绞；好勇不好
xué　　qí bì yě luàn　　hào gāng bú hào xué　　qí bì yě kuáng
学，其蔽也乱；好刚不好学，其蔽也狂。"

【释义】

孔子说："仲由，你听到过六句话的六种弊病吗？"子路回答说："没有。"孔子说："坐下！我告诉你。爱好仁而不爱好学习，其弊病是容易受人愚弄；爱好智而不爱好学习，其弊病是好高骛远而没有基础；重视诚信而不爱好学习，其弊病是反而会被伤害；重视直率而不爱好学习，其弊病是急切而尖刻刺人；爱好勇力而不爱好学习，其弊病是犯上作乱；爱好刚强而不爱好学习，其弊病是狂妄。"

【英译】

The Master asked, "Zhong You (Zi Lu), have you heard of the six sentences and the potential drawbacks related to them?" Zi Lu answered, "No." The Master then said, "Sit down, and I will tell you about them. To love humaneness but not learning, one may easily be deceived; to love wisdom but not learning, one may aim too high yet without any foundation; to value integrity but not learning, one may be hurt by others; to love frankness but not learning, one may sound rash and biting; to love courage but not learning, one may become rebellious against authorities; and to love firmness but not learning, one may become arrogant."

阳货第十七　Chapter Seventeen

The Master said, "*The Book of Songs* can inspire your emotions, and help you observe social and political gains and losses. It can serve as a channel for making friends and for expressing your resentment against the unfair."

17.9
zǐ yuē　　　xiǎo zǐ　　hé mò xué fú　　shī　　　shī kě yǐ xīng
子曰："小子，何莫学夫《诗》？《诗》可以兴，
kě yǐ guān　　kě yǐ qún　　kě yǐ yuàn　　ěr zhī shì fù　　yuǎn zhī shì
可以观，可以群，可以怨。迩之事父，远之事
jūn　　duō shí yú niǎo shòu cǎo mù zhī míng
君。多识于鸟兽草木之名。"

【释义】

孔子说："弟子们，为什么不学习《诗》呢？学《诗》可以即景抒发人的思想感情，可以用来观察民俗民情及政治得失，可以用来交朋友，可以用来讽刺评论不平的事情。近可以用来侍奉父母，远可以用来侍奉君主，还可以多知道一些鸟兽草木的名称。"

【英译】

The Master said, "Young people, why don't you learn *The Book of Songs*? It can inspire your emotions, and help you observe social and political gains and losses. It can serve as a channel for making friends and for expressing your resentment against the unfair. From the book, you can learn ways to serve your parents at home and the ruler at court. Moreover, you can enrich your knowledge in the names of birds and beasts, grass and trees."

Chapter Seventeen 阳货第十七

孔子对孔鲤说:"人如果不学《周南》、《召南》,大概就像面对着墙壁站在那里吧。"

The Master said to his son Bo Yu (Kong Li), "A man without any knowledge of *Zhounan* and *Shaonan* is like a man who stands with his face right against a wall."

17.10
zǐ wèi bó yú yuē   rǔ wéi zhōu nán   shào nán yǐ hū rén
子谓伯鱼曰:"女为《周南》、《召南》矣乎?人
ér bù wéi zhōu nán   shào nán   qí yóu zhèng qiáng miàn ér lì yě
而不为《周南》、《召南》,其犹正 墙 面而立也
yú
与!"

【释义】

孔子对孔鲤说:"你学习《周南》、《召南》了吗?人如果不学《周南》、《召南》,大概就像面对着墙壁站在那里吧。"

【英译】

The Master said to his son Bo Yu (Kong Li), "Have you studied *Zhounan* and *Shaonan*? A man without any knowledge of *Zhounan* and *Shaonan* is like a man who stands with his face right against a wall."

Note: *Zhounan* and *Shaonan* are parts of *The Book of Songs*.

阳货第十七　Chapter Seventeen

【释义】

　　孔子说："总是说礼呀礼呀，难道仅仅是指玉帛之类的礼器而言的吗？总是说乐呀乐呀，难道仅仅是指钟鼓之类的乐器而言的吗？"

【英译】

　　The Master said, "People often mention the word 'ritual', but does ritual only refer to the ceremonial presentation of jade and silk? People often mention the word 'music', but does music only refer to the sound made by such musical instruments as bells and drums?"

孔子说："总是说礼呀礼呀，难道仅仅是指玉帛之类的礼器而言的吗？总是说乐呀乐呀，难道仅仅是指钟鼓之类的乐器而言的吗？"

The Master said, "People often mention the word 'ritual', but does ritual only refer to the ceremonial presentation of jade and silk? People often mention the word 'music', but does music only refer to the sound made by such instruments as bells and drums?"

17.11
zǐ yuē　　　　lǐ yún lǐ yún　　yù bó yún hū zāi　　yuè yún yuè yún
子曰："礼云礼云，玉帛云乎哉？乐云乐云，
zhōng gǔ yún hū zāi
钟　鼓云乎哉？"

Chapter Seventeen 阳货第十七

孔子说:"外表严厉而内心怯弱,若用小人作比喻,大概就像是穿壁、翻墙行窃的小偷吧。"

The Master said, "A man who is firm in appearance but timid inside is a petty-minded man. He is like a burglar who steals by breaking through or climbing over a wall."

【释义】

孔子说:"外表严厉而内心怯弱,若用小人作比喻,大概就像是穿壁、翻墙行窃的小偷吧。"

【英译】

The Master said, "A man who is firm in appearance but timid inside is a petty-minded man. He is like a burglar who steals by breaking through or climbing over a wall."

17.12 子曰:"色厉而内荏,譬诸小人,其犹穿窬之盗也与?"

阳货第十七　Chapter Seventeen

孔子说："那种谁也不得罪的好好先生是败坏道德的人。"

The Master said, "Those who flatter and associate with evil people yet try to offend no one are pests of virtue."

【释义】

孔子说："那种谁也不得罪的好好先生是败坏道德的人。"

【英译】

The Master said, "Those who flatter and associate with evil people yet try to offend no one are pests of virtue."

17.13
zǐ yuē　　　xiāng yuàn　　dé zhī zéi yě
子曰："乡原，德之贼也。"

Chapter Seventeen 阳货第十七

孔子说:"拿在路上听到的传言到处传播,是对道德的背弃。"

The Master said, "To spread rumors one hears on the way is to go against virtue."

【释义】

孔子说:"拿在路上听到的传言到处传播,是对道德的背弃。"

【英译】

The Master said, "To spread rumors one hears on the way is to go against virtue."

17.14
zǐ yuē　　　dào tīng ér tú shuō　　dé zhī qì yě
子曰:"道听而涂说,德之弃也。"

219

阳货第十七　Chapter Seventeen

孔子说："道德品质恶劣的人总担心得不到官位；已经得到之后，又担心失掉。如果他担心失掉官位，那就什么都干得出来了。"

The Master said, "For a morally degenerated man, before he gets what he desires, he is concerned about not being able to get it; after he gets it, he then is concerned about losing it. If a man is obsessive about what he may lose, then he may stop at nothing in order to retain what he has obtained."

17.15
zǐ yuē　　　　　bǐ fū kě yǔ shì jūn yě yú zāi　　qí wèi dé zhī yě
子曰："鄙夫可与事君也与哉？其未得之也，
huàn dé zhī　　jì dé zhī　　huàn shī zhī　　gǒu huàn shī zhī　　wú suǒ bú
患得之；既得之，患失之。苟患失之，无所不
zhì yǐ
至矣。"

【释义】

孔子说："可以和一个道德品质恶劣的人一起侍奉君主吗？他在没有得到官位时，总担心得不到；已经得到之后，又担心失掉。如果他担心失掉官位，那就什么都干得出来了。"

【英译】

The Master said, "How can one serve the ruler along with a morally degenerated man? Before he gets what he desires, he is concerned about not being able to get it; after he gets it, he then is concerned about losing it. If a man is obsessive about what he may lose, then he may stop at nothing in order to retain what he has obtained."

Chapter Seventeen 阳货第十七

孔子说:"古代的狂者任意直言,现在的狂者就放荡不羁了。"

The Master said, "In ancient times, the common people had three failings, but now even these failings seem hard to find."

17.16
子曰:"古者民有三疾,今也或是之亡也。古之狂也肆,今之狂也荡;古之矜也廉,今之矜也忿戾;古之愚也直,今之愚也诈而已矣。"

【释义】

孔子说:"古人有三种毛病,现在的人或许连这也没有了。古代的狂者任意直言,现在的狂者就放荡不羁了;古代自傲的人为人严厉难以接近,现在自傲的人就常发怒和蛮不讲理;古代愚笨的人常自作主张,现在愚笨的人却只是欺诈而已。"

【英译】

The Master said, "In ancient times, the common people had three failings, but now even these failings seem hard to find. In ancient times, the presumptuous were courageous, but today, they are unrestrained; in ancient times, the self-conceited were stern, but today, they are irritable and perverse; in ancient times, the foolish were straightforward, but now they have become deceptive."

阳货第十七　Chapter Seventeen

孔子说："花言巧语、满脸都是伪善的人，是没有什么仁德的。"

The Master said, "Flattery words and ingratiating attitude are signs of lack of virtue."

【释义】

孔子说："花言巧语、满脸都是伪善的人，是没有什么仁德的。"

【英译】

The Master said, "Flattery words and ingratiating attitude are signs of lack of virtue."

17.17 zǐ yuē　　　qiǎo yán lìng sè　　xiǎn yǐ rén
子曰："巧言令色，鲜矣仁。"

Chapter Seventeen 阳货第十七

孔子说:"我厌恶用紫色取代了红色,厌恶用郑国的曲调扰乱了雅乐的正统音调,厌恶用巧口俐辩倾覆国家的人。"

The Master said, "I hate the replacement of vermillion with purple. I hate the replacement of elegant music with the pop music of the Zheng State. And I hate people using clever talks to subvert other people's state or fief."

【释义】

孔子说:"我厌恶用紫色取代了红色,厌恶用郑国的曲调扰乱了雅乐的正统音调,厌恶用巧口俐辩倾覆国家的人。"

【英译】

The Master said, "I hate the replacement of vermillion with purple. I hate the replacement of elegant music with the pop music of the Zheng State. And I hate people using clever talks to subvert other people's state or fief."

17.18
zǐ yuē　　wù zǐ zhī duó zhū yě　　wù zhèng shēng zhī luàn yǎ yuè yě
子曰:"恶紫之夺朱也,恶郑声之乱雅乐也,
wù lì kǒu zhī fù bāng jiā zhě
恶利口之覆邦家者。"

阳货第十七　Chapter Seventeen

孔子说："天说了什么了吗？春夏秋冬照样运行，万物照样生长。"

The Master said, "Has Heaven ever said anything? Yet the four seasons follow their due course, and all things on earth continue to grow."

17.19
zǐ yuē　　　　yú yù wú yán　　　　zǐ gòng yuē　　　zǐ rú bù yán
子曰："予欲无言。"子贡曰："子如不言，
zé xiǎo zǐ hé shù yān　　zǐ yuē　　tiān hé yán zāi　sì shí xíng
则小子何述焉？"子曰："天何言哉？四时行
yān　　bǎi wù shēng yān　　tiān hé yán zāi
焉，百物生焉，天何言哉？"

【释义】

孔子说："我不想实行言教了。"子贡说："老师如果不实行言教，那我们传述什么呢？"孔子说："天说了什么了吗？春夏秋冬照样运行，万物照样生长，天说了什么了吗？"

【英译】

The Master said, "I'd prefer not to speak." Zi Gong asked, "If you don't speak, what shall we the disciples record?" The Master answered, "Has Heaven ever said anything? Yet the four seasons follow their due course, and all things on earth continue to grow. Has Heaven ever said anything?"

Chapter Seventeen 阳货第十七

孺悲想见孔子，孔子托辞有病加以拒绝。传口信的人刚出门，孔子就拿过瑟弹着唱歌，故意让传口信的人听到。

Ru Bei wished to see Confucius, but the Master refused to see him by the excuse of being unwell. However, immediately after the messenger went out of the gate, the Master took his *se* and sang to the music, for the very purpose of being heard by the messenger.

17.20

rú bēi yù jiàn kǒng zǐ　　kǒng zǐ cí yǐ jí　　jiāng mìng zhě chū hù
孺 悲 欲 见 孔 子， 孔 子 辞 以 疾。 将 命 者 出 户，
qǔ sè ér gē　　shǐ zhī wén zhī
取 瑟 而 歌， 使 之 闻 之。

【释义】

孺悲想见孔子，孔子托辞有病加以拒绝。传口信的人刚出门，孔子就拿过瑟弹着唱歌，故意让传口信的人听到。

【英译】

Ru Bei wished to see Confucius, but the Master refused to see him by the excuse of being unwell. However, immediately after the messenger went out of the gate, the Master took his *se* and sang to the music, for the very purpose of being heard by the messenger.

225

阳货第十七　Chapter Seventeen

孔子说："三年的守丧期，为天下通行的丧礼。"

The Master said, "Three years' mourning for one's parents is a universal practice."

17.21 宰我问："三年之丧，期已久矣。君子三年不为礼，礼必坏；三年不为乐，乐必崩。旧谷既没，新谷既升，钻燧改火，期可已矣。"子曰："食夫稻，衣夫锦，于女安乎？"曰："安。"

【释义】

宰我问道："为父母守丧三年，为期太久。君子三年不习礼，礼一定会败坏；三年不奏乐，乐一定会毁掉。陈谷已经吃完，新谷已经成熟，钻火所用的木材已经过了一个轮回，丧期满一年也就可以了。"孔子说："那么吃白米饭，穿花缎衣，对于你来说能心安吗？"宰我说："心安。"

【英译】

Zai Wo (Zai Yu) said, "The three-year mourning period for one's parents is too long. For a man of virtue, if he does not practice rituals during three years, then the rituals will be discarded; if he does not play music during three years, then the music will be discarded. The old grains will be eaten out and new grains will come for the rescue. The wood used for charcoal is changed on a yearly basis. So a year's mourning seems enough." The Master asked, "Can your mind be at ease if you start to eat rice and wear silk after one year's time?" Zai Wo answered yes.

Chapter Seventeen 阳货第十七

"女安，则为之！夫君子之居丧，食旨不甘，闻乐不乐，居处不安，故不为也。今女安，则为之！"

宰我出，子曰："予之不仁也！子生三年，然后免于父母之怀。夫三年之丧，天下之通丧也。予也有三年之爱于其父母乎？"

【释义】

孔子说："你只要心安，就那样做吧！君子服丧期间，吃美味不觉得甘美，听音乐不觉得快乐，闲居也不觉得安适，因此不那样做。现在你心安，就那样做吧！"

宰我出去了。孔子说："宰予不仁啊！子女生下三年，然后才脱离父母的怀抱。三年的守丧期，为天下通行的丧礼。宰予不也是从他父母那里享有三年怀抱的爱抚吗？"

【英译】

The Master said, "As long as as your mind is at ease, you can do that. A man of virtue who is in mourning would not do that, because he can't enjoy the food even if he is served delicacies, he can't feel the joy even if he listens to music, and he doesn't feel comfortable even if he leads a life of leasure. As long as your mind is at ease, you can do that."

After Zai Wo left, the Master said, "Zai Yu is lack of virtue. A child only leaves his parents' arms after he is three years old. Three years' mourning for one's parents is a universal practice. Didn't Zai Yu enjoy three years' love in his parents' arms?"

阳货第十七　Chapter Seventeen

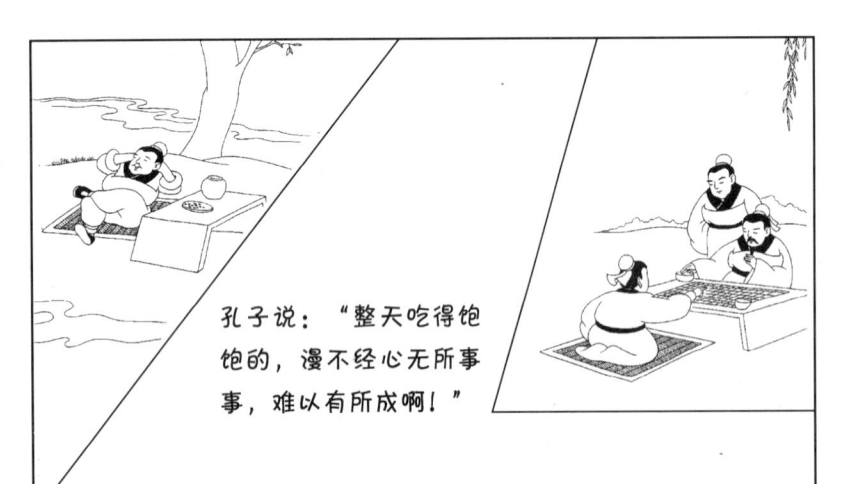

【释义】

孔子说:"整天吃得饱饱的,漫不经心无所事事,难以有所成啊!不是有六博和围棋的游戏吗?玩玩儿棋也比闲着混日子强。"

【英译】

The Master said, "For a man who eats to his heart's content and idles around every day, it is hard to achieve anything. Aren't there chess games? Even playing chess games is better than aimlessly drifting along."

17.22
zǐ yuē　　bǎo shí zhōng rì　wú suǒ yòng xīn　nán yǐ zāi　bù
子曰:"饱食终日,无所用心,难矣哉!不
yǒu bó yì zhě hū　wéi zhī　yóu xián hū yǐ
有博弈者乎,为之,犹贤乎已。"

Chapter Seventeen 阳货第十七

【释义】

子路问道:"君子尊崇勇敢吗?"孔子说:"君子认为义是最值得尊崇的。君子只有勇敢而没有道义,就会犯上作乱;小人只有勇敢而没有道义,就会成为强盗。"

【英译】

Zi Lu asked, "Does a man of virtue advocate bravery?" The Master answered, "A man of virtue prioritizes righteousness. For a man of virtue, bravery without the restraint of righteousness may lead to rebellion against the authorities; for a petty-minded man, bravery without the restraint of righteousness may lead to acts of burglary."

17.23
zǐ lù yuē jūn zǐ shàng yǒng hū zǐ yuē jūn zǐ yì yǐ
子路曰:"君子尚勇乎?"子曰:"君子义以
wéi shàng jūn zǐ yǒu yǒng ér wú yì wéi luàn xiǎo rén yǒu yǒng ér wú yì
为上。君子有勇而无义为乱,小人有勇而无义
wéi dào
为盗。"

阳货第十七　Chapter Seventeen

孔子说："君子厌恶到处宣扬别人坏处的人，厌恶身居下位却毁谤上位的人，厌恶勇敢却不懂礼仪的人，厌恶果断敢为却头脑僵化的人。"

The Master said, "A man of virtue detests those who spread the demerits of other people, those who are lower in rank or position but speak ill of their seniors, those who are courageous but not observant of etiquette, and those who are resolute but stubborn."

17.24
zǐ gòng yuē　　　jūn zǐ yì yǒu wù hū　　zǐ yuē　　yǒu wù
子贡曰："君子亦有恶乎？"子曰："有恶。
wù chēng rén zhī è zhě　wù jū xià liú ér shàn shàng zhě　wù yǒng ér wú
恶称人之恶者，恶居下流而讪上者，恶勇而无
lǐ zhě　　wù guǒ gǎn ér zhì zhě　　yuē　　cì yě yì yǒu wù hū
礼者，恶果敢而窒者。"曰："赐也亦有恶乎？"
wù jiāo yǐ wéi zhì zhě　wù bú xùn yǐ wéi yǒng zhě　wù jié yǐ wéi
"恶徼以为知者，恶不孙以为勇者，恶讦以为
zhí zhě
直者。"

【释义】

子贡问道："君子也有厌恶的吗？"孔子说："有厌恶的。厌恶到处宣扬别人坏处的人，厌恶身居下位却毁谤上位的人，厌恶勇敢却不懂礼仪的人，厌恶果断敢为却头脑僵化的人。"孔子又说："赐，你也有厌恶的吗？"子贡说："我厌恶抄袭了别人的成绩却当做自己的聪明的人，厌恶不谦虚却以为自己很勇敢的人，厌恶揭发别人却以为自己很正直的人。"

【英译】

Zi Gong asked, "Are there things that a man of virtue detests?" The Master answered, "Yes. A man of virtue detests those who spread the demerits of other people, those who are lower in rank or position but speak ill of their seniors, those who are courageous but not observant of etiquette, and those who are resolute but stubborn." The Master then asked, "Ci, are there things that you detest?" Zi Gong answered, "Yes. I detest those who practice plagiarism and yet regard themselves as learned. I detest those who are arrogant and rude and yet regard themselves as courageous. And I detest those who enjoy exposing others' faults and yet regard themselves as candid."

Chapter Seventeen 阳货第十七

孔子说："只有女子和小人最难养用，稍有亲近就放肆，稍有疏远就抱怨。"

The Master said, "Only women and petty-minded men are hard to get along. They become impertinent when treated in an intimate manner and take offense when kept at a distance."

【释义】

孔子说："只有女子和小人最难养用。稍有亲近就放肆，稍有疏远就抱怨。"

【英译】

The Master said, "Only women and petty-minded men are hard to get along. They become impertinent when treated in an intimate manner and take offense when kept at a distance."

17.25 zǐ yuē wéi nǚ zǐ yǔ xiǎo rén wéi nán yǎng yě   jìn zhī zé bú xùn
子曰："唯女子与小人为难养也。近之则不孙，
yuǎn zhī zé yuàn
远之则怨。"

231

阳货第十七　Chapter Seventeen

孔子说："人活到四十岁还被人厌恶，那他这一辈子就算完了啊！"

The Master said, "For a man who has reached the age of 40 and is still detested by other people, it is impossible for him to achieve anything."

【释义】

孔子说："人活到四十岁还被人厌恶，那他这一辈子就算完了啊！"

【英译】

The Master said, "For a man who has reached the age of 40 and is still detested by other people, it is impossible for him to achieve anything."

17.26
zǐ yuē　　nián sì shí ér jiàn wù yān　qí zhōng yě yǐ
子曰："年四十而见恶焉，其终也已。"

wēi zǐ dì shí bā
微子第十八
CHAPTER EIGHTEEN

微子第十八　Chapter Eighteen

孔子说："殷朝有三位仁人。"

The Master said, "The Shang Dynasty boasted three role models of men of virtue."

18.1
wēi zǐ qù zhī　jī zǐ wéi zhī nú　bǐ gān jiàn ér sǐ　kǒng zǐ
微子去之，箕子为之奴，比干谏而死。孔子
yuē　yīn yǒu sān rén yān
曰："殷有三仁焉。"

【释义】

微子离开了纣王，箕子做了他的奴隶，比干强谏而被杀。孔子说："殷朝有三位仁人。"

【英译】

(King Zhou of the Shang Dynasty was a tyrant. As a result,) Weizi left the country, Ji Zi was made a slave, and Bi Gan was killed because of his remonstration of the king. The Master said, "The Shang Dynasty boasted three role models of men of virtue."

Note: Weizi, half brother of King Zhou, left the country after his repeated remonstration of the king was unheeded. Ji Zi was an uncle of King Zhou. After his remonstration was rejected, he feigned madness to save his own life, but was condemned to a slave. Bi Gan was an uncle of King Zhou. His repeated reprimand angered King Zhou, who killed him by extracting his heart.

Chapter Eighteen 微子第十八

Liuxia Hui said, "If I insist on serving people in an upright way, where else can I avoid the experience of being dismissed? If I agreed to compromise my principle and served people in a crooked way, then what's the need of leaving my native land?"

18.2
liǔ xià huì wéi shì shī　　sān chù　　rén yuē　　zǐ wèi kě yǐ qù hū
柳下惠为士师，三黜。人曰："子未可以去乎？"
yuē　　zhí dào ér shì rén　　yān wǎng ér bù sān chù　　wǎng dào ér shì
曰："直道而事人，焉往而不三黜？枉道而事
rén　　hé bì qù fù mǔ zhī bāng
人，何必去父母之邦？"

【释义】

柳下惠做司法官，多次被罢免。有人对他说："您不可以离开吗？"柳下惠说："以正直之道来侍奉人，到哪里不会被多次罢免呢？以邪曲之道侍奉人，又何必离开自己的国家呢？"

【英译】

Liuxia Hui served as a criminal judge, and for three times he was dismissed from office. Someone said to him, "Why don't you leave this place to look for another position?" Liuxia Hui answered, "If I insist on serving people in an upright way, where else can I avoid the experience of being dismissed? If I agreed to compromise my principle and served people in a crooked way, then what's the need of leaving my native land?"

微子第十八　Chapter Eighteen

【释义】

齐景公准备给孔子以礼遇留住他，说："像季氏那样的地位，我不能给；将用季氏、孟氏之间的待遇来安置他。"孔子说："我已经老了，不能做什么了。"孔子于是离开了齐国。

【英译】

Duke Jing of the Qi State decided to treat the Master with courtesy and to keep him in the state. In terms of the treatment for the Master, he said, "I can't treat him in the same way as I treat the head of the Ji family. His treatment should be between what is accorded to the head of the Ji family and what is accorded to the head of the Meng family." The Master said, "I am too old to be of any use." With that, he left the State of Qi.

Duke Jing of the Qi State was not sincere in keeping Confucius, so the Master left Qi.

18.3
qí jǐng gōng dài kǒng zǐ　　yuē　　ruò jì shì　　zé wú bù néng　　yǐ
齐景公待孔子，曰："若季氏，则吾不能，以
jì mèng zhī jiān dài zhī　　yuē　　wú lǎo yǐ　　bù néng yòng yě
季孟之间待之。"曰："吾老矣，不能用也。"
kǒng zǐ xíng
孔子行。

Chapter Eighteen 微子第十八

齐国送给鲁君一些歌伎舞女，当政的季桓子接受了，三天不举行朝礼以治政事。孔子于是离开了鲁国。

The State of Qi sent to the ruler of the State of Lu some sing-song girls as a gift. Ji Huanzi, the Chief Minister, accepted, and for three days after that he held no court to discuss state affairs. Seeing this, the Master left the State of Lu.

【释义】

齐国送给鲁君一些歌伎舞女，当政的季桓子接受了，三天不举行朝礼以治政事。孔子于是离开了鲁国。

【英译】

The State of Qi sent to the ruler of the State of Lu some sing-song girls as a gift. Ji Huanzi, the Chief Minister, accepted, and for three days after that he held no court to discuss state affairs. Seeing this, the Master left the State of Lu.

18.4　qí rén kuì nǚ yuè　jì huán zǐ shòu zhī　sān rì bù cháo　kǒng zǐ xíng
齐人归女乐，季桓子受之，三日不朝。孔子行。

微子第十八　Chapter Eighteen

楚国的狂人接舆，唱着歌从孔子车旁经过，他唱道："凤呀！凤呀！为什么你的德行竟如此衰败！以往的错事已不可制止，未来的前途还来得及深谋于怀。"

The "madman of Chu" Jie Yu passed by Confucius' carriage while singing, "Phoenix! Phoenix! Why is your virtue so declined? Past wrongs can not be stopped, but the future can still be planned on."

【释义】

楚国的狂人接舆，唱着歌从孔子车旁经过，他唱道："凤呀！凤呀！为什么你的德行竟如此衰败！以往的错事已不可制止，未来的前途还来得及深谋于怀。算了吧！算了吧！当今的从政者岌岌可危啊！"

孔子下车，想跟他讲话。他急行避开，孔子终不能跟他讲话。

【英译】

The "madman of Chu" Jie Yu passed by Confucius' carriage while singing, "Phoenix! Phoenix! Why is your virtue so declined? Past wrongs can not be stopped, but the future can still be planned on. Give it up! Give it up! The rulers today are in great danger!"

The Master got off the carriage and wished to talk to him, but Jie Yu hurried away, so the Master wasn't able to talk to him.

18.5
chǔ kuáng jiē yú gē ér guò kǒng zǐ yuē　fèng xī fèng xī hé dé zhī
楚 狂 接 舆 歌 而 过 孔 子 曰："凤 兮 凤 兮！何 德 之
shuāi　wǎng zhě bù kě jiàn　lái zhě yóu kě zhuī　yǐ ér　yǐ ér
衰？往 者 不 可 谏，来 者 犹 可 追。已 而！已 而！
jīn zhī cóng zhèng zhě dài ér
今 之 从 政 者 殆 而！"
kǒng zǐ xià　yù yǔ zhī yán　qū ér bì zhī　bù dé yǔ zhī yán
孔 子 下，欲 与 之 言。趋 而 避 之，不 得 与 之 言。

Chapter Eighteen   微子第十八

孔子怅然若失地说："人是不能同鸟兽同群的，我不同世上这些人同群又和谁同群呢？"

The Master said with a sigh, "We can not associate with birds and beasts because they are different from us. Who else can I associate with other than people in the world?"

18.6
cháng jū jié nì ǒu ér gēng kǒng zǐ guò zhī shǐ zǐ lù wèn jīn yān
长沮、桀溺耦而耕，孔子过之，使子路问津焉。
cháng jū yuē fú zhí yú zhě wéi shuí zǐ lù yuē wéi kǒng
长沮曰："夫执舆者为谁？"子路曰："为孔
qiū yuē shì lǔ kǒng qiū yú yuē shì yě yuē
丘。"曰："是鲁孔丘与？"曰："是也。"曰：
shì zhī jīn yǐ
"是知津矣。"
wèn yú jié nì jié nì yuē zǐ wéi shuí yuē wéi zhòng
问于桀溺。桀溺曰："子为谁？"曰："为仲
yóu yuē shì lǔ kǒng qiū zhī tú yú duì yuē rán
由。"曰："是鲁孔丘之徒与？"对曰："然。"

【释义】
　　长沮、桀溺在一起耕种，孔子路过，叫子路去问渡口在那里。
　　长沮说："那个拿着缰绳的是谁？"子路说："是孔丘。"长沮说："是鲁国的孔丘吗？"子路说："是的。"长沮说："那他是知道渡口在哪里的了。"
　　子路再去问桀溺。桀溺说："你是谁？"子路说："是仲由。"桀溺说："是鲁国孔丘的门徒吗？"子路回答："是的。"

【英译】
　　Chang Ju and Jie Ni were plowing the field alongside each other. When the Master and his disciples were passing by, he sent Zi Lu to ask about the ford.
　　Chang Ju asked, "Who's that man holding the reins in the carriage?" Zi Lu answered, "Confucius." Chang Ju asked, "Confucius from the State of Lu?" Zi Lu said yes. Chang Ju then said, "In this case, he should know the ford."
　　Zi Lu turned to Jie Ni for help. Jie Ni asked, "Who are you?" "Zhong You (Zi Lu)." was the answer. Jie Ni said, "You must be a disciple of Confucius of the State of Lu." Zi Lu said yes.

微子第十八　Chapter Eighteen

曰："滔滔者天下皆是也，而谁以易之？且而与其从辟人之士也，岂若从辟世之士哉？"耰而不辍。子路行以告。夫子怃然曰："鸟兽不可与同群，吾非斯人之徒与而谁与？天下有道，丘不与易也。"

【释义】

桀溺说："现在不合理的坏事像滔滔大水，到处都是，和谁去改变它呀？而且你与其跟着躲避人的人，何不跟着逃避社会的人呢？"说完，不停地干他的活。

子路回来把情形报告了孔子。孔子怅然若失地说："人是不能同鸟兽同群的，我不同世上这些人同群又和谁同群呢？如果天下有道，我也不会同他们一起来改变它了。"

【英译】

Then Jie Ni said, "The whole world is in chaos. Who can you work along to change the situation? Rather than following someone who tries to shun evil people, wouldn't it be better to follow those who shun the world?" After having said this, he resumed his work and busied himself covering up the seeds with mud.

Zi Lu came back and reported to Confucius what the two people had said. The Master said with a sigh, "We can not associate with birds and beasts because they are different from us. Who else can I associate with other than people in the world? If the Way prevailed, there would be no need for me to work with others to change the situation."

Chapter Eighteen 微子第十八

子路说："君子做官，只是为了实行君臣之义。至于道的行不通，这是已经知道的了。"

Zi Lu said, "For a man of virtue, to hold office is to fulfill his duty towards the sovereign. As for the fact that the Way does not prevail, it is already known."

18.7

zǐ lù cóng ér hòu, yù zhàng rén, yǐ zhàng hè diào
子路从而后，遇丈人，以杖荷蓧。

zǐ lù wèn yuē: "zǐ jiàn fū zǐ hū?" zhàng rén yuē: "sì tǐ
子路问曰："子见夫子乎？"丈人曰："四体

bù qín, wǔ gǔ bù fēn, shú wéi fū zǐ?" zhí qí zhàng ér yún.
不勤，五谷不分，孰为夫子？"植其杖而芸。

zǐ lù gǒng ér lì.
子路拱而立。

zhǐ zǐ lù sù, shā jī wéi shǔ ér sì zhī, jiàn qí èr zǐ yān.
止子路宿，杀鸡为黍而食之，见其二子焉。

【释义】

子路跟随孔子周游，有一次落在后面，碰到一位老人，用拐杖扛着除草农具。

子路问道："您见到我的老师了吗？"老人说："你们这些人四肢不勤劳，五谷分不清，谁是老师？"于是就把拐杖插在地上除起草来。子路一直拱着手恭敬地站在那里。

老人便留子路住宿，忙着杀鸡做饭给他食用，还引出自己的两个儿子见了子路。

【英译】

Zi Lu was travelling around with Confucius. Once he fell behind and met an old man who used a stick to carry his weeding tools.

Zi Lu asked, "Excuse me, but have you seen my teacher?" The old man answered, "Among you people who do not work with your limbs and who can not tell one kind of grain from another, who is the teacher?" With that, he planted his stick into the field and started to weed. Zi Lu stood by, with his hands folded in front of his chest, to show his respect.

The old man put Zi Lu up for the night, and cooked a freshly killed chicken and some millet to treat his guest. He also introduced his two sons to him.

微子第十八　Chapter Eighteen

明日，子路行以告。
子曰："隐者也。"使子路反见之。至则行矣。
子路曰："不仕无义。长幼之节，不可废也；君臣之义，如之何其废之？欲洁其身，而乱大伦。君子之仕也，行其义也。道之不行，已知之矣。"

【释义】

第二天，子路赶上了孔子，把自己的经历告诉了孔子。

孔子说："这是一位隐士。"让子路返回去见他。子路到了他家，他已出门了。

子路说："不做官是不合乎义的。长幼之间的礼节不能废弃；君臣之间的大义，怎么能废弃呢？想要自己清白，却破坏了根本的伦理关系。君子做官，只是为了实行君臣之义。至于道的行不通，这是已经知道的了。"

【英译】

The next day, Zi Lu caught up with his teacher and told him what had happened.

The Master said "He is a recluse." and sent Zi Lu back to visit the old man. When Zi Lu arrived at the place, the old man had already left.

Zi Lu remarked, "Not to hold office is not in accord with righteousness. Since the relationship between the old and the young can not be ignored, how can one ignore the duties one has towards the sovereign? To maintain one's own purity is at the cost of the proper ethics. For a man of virtue, to hold office is to fulfill his duty towards the sovereign. As for the fact that the Way does not prevail, it is already known."

Chapter Eighteen 微子第十八

> 孔子说："没有什么可以的，也没有什么不可以的。"
>
> The Master said, "There is no definite rule about what should be done and what shouldn't be done."

18.8
逸民：伯夷、叔齐、虞仲、夷逸、朱张、柳下惠、少连。子曰："不降其志，不辱其身，伯夷、叔齐与！"谓："柳下惠、少连，降志辱身矣，言中伦，行中虑，其斯而已矣。"谓："虞仲、夷逸，隐居放言，身中清，废中权。我则异于是，无可无不可。"

【释义】

遗落民间的贤者有：伯夷、叔齐、虞仲、夷逸、朱张、柳下惠、少连。孔子说："不降低自己的志向，不玷辱自己的人格，这样的人是伯夷、叔齐吧？"又说："柳下惠、少连这两个人，降低了志向，玷辱了人格，但是讲话有伦次，做事有谋虑，他们不过如此罢了。"又说："虞仲、夷逸这两个人，避世隐居，放肆敢言，修身合乎清廉，弃官合乎权宜。我则跟这些人不同，没有什么可以的，也没有什么不可以的。"

【英译】

People who had retired to seclusion were Bo Yi, Shu Qi, Yu Zhong, Yi Yi, Zhu Zhang, Liuxia Hui and Shao Lian. The Master said, "Bo Yi and Shu Qi refused to lower their aspirations, nor disgrace their integrity." He also said, "While Liuxia Hui and Shao Lian lowered their aspirations and suffered disgrace, they spoke in appropriate terms and act with prudence. This is all that can be said about them." The Master also said, "Yu Zhong and Yi Yi lived in seclusion and spoke their mind freely. They retained purity of characters by living a secluded life and practiced expediency by withdrawing from official positions. I am different from all these people. For me, there is no definite rule about what should be done and what shouldn't be done."

243

微子第十八　Chapter Eighteen

鲁国的太师名叫挚的到了齐国，二饭乐师名叫干的到了楚国。

The Lu State's chief musician Zhi left for Qi; Gan, the musician playing for the second course left for Chu.

【释义】

鲁国的太师名叫挚的到了齐国，二饭乐师名叫干的到了楚国，三饭乐师名叫缭的到了蔡国，四饭乐师名叫缺的到了秦国。鼓手名叫方叔的人到了黄河之滨，摇小鼓的名叫武的人到了汉水之滨，少师名叫阳的以及击磬师名叫襄的人到了海边。

【英译】

(The Lu State was on the wane and rituals and music were ignored.) The Lu State's chief musician Zhi left for Qi; Gan, the musician playing for the second course left for Chu; Liao, the musician playing for the third course left for Cai; Que, the musician playing the fourth course left for Qin; Fang Shu, the drummer, left and settled by the Yellow River; Wu, the hand-drum player, left and settled by the Han River; Yang, the assistant musician, and Xiang, the chiming bells player, left to live by the seaside.

Note: In ancient times, it was customary for rulers to have their meals with the accompaniment of music. Different musicians played at different courses.

18.9
tài shī zhì shì qí　yà fàn gān shì chǔ　sān fàn liáo shì cài　sì fàn
太师挚适齐，亚饭干适楚，三饭缭适蔡，四饭
quē shì qín　gǔ fāng shū rù yú hé　bō táo wǔ rù yú hàn　shào shī
缺适秦。鼓方叔入于河，播鼗武入于汉，少师
yáng　jī qìng xiāng rù yú hǎi
阳、击磬襄入于海。

Chapter Eighteen 微子第十八

周公对鲁公说:"君子不怠慢他的亲族,不让大臣埋怨没有被任用。故友旧交没有重大过失,就不遗弃他们。对别人不求全责备。"

Duke Zhou said to his son Duke Lu, "A man of virtue does not distance himself from his relatives, nor does he cause his ministers to complain about being ignored. For people who have served you for a long time, do not dismiss them unless they make severe mistakes. Do not demand perfection of anyone."

18.10 zhōu gōng wèi lǔ gōng yuē　jūn zǐ bù chí qí qīn　bù shǐ dà chén yuàn hū bù yǐ　gù jiù wú dà gù　zé bú qì yě　wú qiú bèi yú yì rén

周公谓鲁公曰:"君子不施其亲,不使大臣怨乎不以。故旧无大故,则不弃也。无求备于一人。"

【释义】

周公对鲁公说:"君子不怠慢他的亲族,不让大臣埋怨没有被任用。故友旧交没有重大过失,就不遗弃他们。对别人不求全责备。"

【英译】

Duke Zhou said to his son Duke Lu, "A man of virtue does not distance himself from his relatives, nor does he cause his ministers to complain about being ignored. For people who have served you for a long time, do not dismiss them unless they make severe mistakes. Do not demand perfection of anyone."

微子第十八　Chapter Eighteen

周朝有八个知名之士：伯达、伯适、仲突、仲忽、叔夜、叔夏、季随、季骗。

There were eight renowned scholars during the Zhou Dynasty; they are Bo Da, Bo Kuo, Zhong Tu, Zhong Hu, Shu Ye, Shu Xia, Ji Sui, and Ji Gua.

【释义】

周朝有八个知名之士：伯达、伯适、仲突、仲忽、叔夜、叔夏、季随、季骗。

【英译】

There were eight renowned scholars during the Zhou Dynasty; they are Bo Da, Bo Kuo, Zhong Tu, Zhong Hu, Shu Ye, Shu Xia, Ji Sui, and Ji Gua.

18.11
zhōu yǒu bā shì　bó dá　bó kuò　zhòng tū　zhòng hū　shū yè
周有八士：伯达、伯适、仲突、仲忽、叔夜、
shū xià　jì suí　jì guā
叔夏、季随、季骗。

子张第十九

CHAPTER NINETEEN

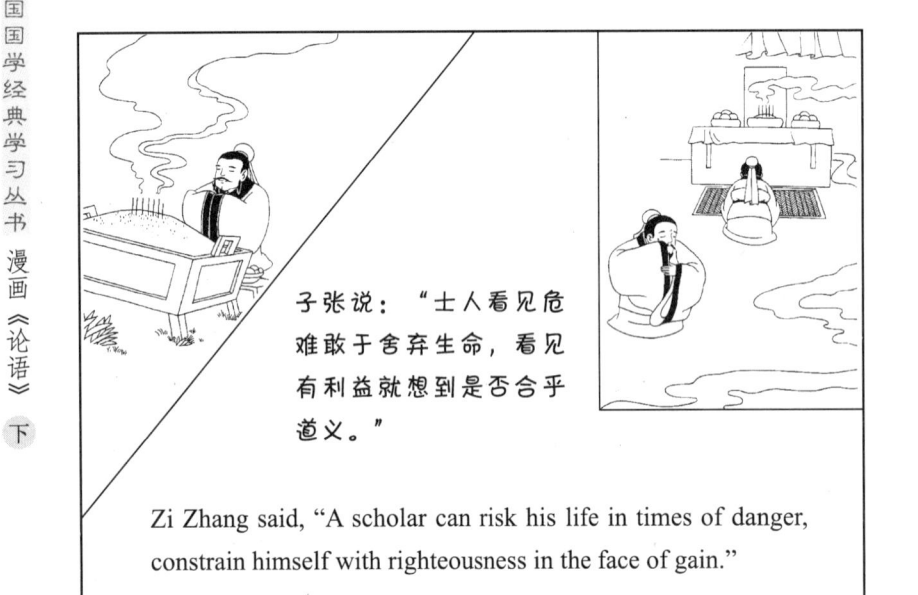

子张第十九　Chapter Nineteen

【释义】

子张说:"士人看见危难敢于舍弃生命,看见有利益就想到是否合乎道义,祭祀的时候要严肃恭敬,居丧的时候要悲哀,这样也就可以了。"

【英译】

Zi Zhang said, "A scholar can risk his life in times of danger, constrain himself with righteousness in the face of gain, act deferentially at sacrificial ceremonies and remain sorrowful at funerals, then it is good enough."

子张说:"士人看见危难敢于舍弃生命,看见有利益就想到是否合乎道义。"

Zi Zhang said, "A scholar can risk his life in times of danger, constrain himself with righteousness in the face of gain."

19.1
zǐ zhāng yuē　　shì jiàn wēi zhì mìng　jiàn dé sī yì　jì sī jìng
子张曰:"士见危致命,见得思义,祭思敬,
sāng sī āi　qí kě yǐ yǐ
丧思哀,其可已矣。"

Chapter Nineteen　子张第十九

子张说："执守道德而不能发扬光大，信仰道义而不能坚持，这怎么能算是有道德？又怎么能算是没有道德？"

Zi Zhang said, "How can a man be counted as being virtuous if he holds fast to virtue but can not enhance it, or if he believes in morality and justice but not in a sincere way? How can he be counted as being virtuous?"

【释义】

子张说："执守道德而不能发扬光大，信仰道义而不能坚持，这怎么能算是有道德？又怎么能算是没有道德？"

【英译】

Zi Zhang said, "How can a man be counted as being virtuous if he holds fast to virtue but can not enhance it, or if he believes in morality and justice but not in a sincere way? How can he be counted as being virtuous?"

19.2　
zǐ zhāng yuē　　zhí dé bù hóng　xìn dào bù dǔ　　yān néng wéi yǒu
子　张　曰："执　德　不　弘，信　道　不　笃，焉　能　为　有？
yān néng wéi wú
焉　能　为　亡？"

249

子张说:"君子尊重贤人,也包容广大的普通人;赞美好人,也同情无能的人。"

Zi Zhang said, "A man of virtue respects the virtuous, but at the same time tolerates the ordinary; he compliments on the good, but at the same time sympathizes with the less capable."

19.3 子夏之门人问交于子张。子张曰:"子夏云何?"对曰:"子夏曰:'可者与之,其不可者拒之。'"子张曰:"异乎吾所闻:君子尊贤而容众,嘉善而矜不能。我之大贤与,于人何所不容?我之不贤与,人将拒我,如之何其拒人也?"

【释义】

子夏的弟子向子张问怎样与人交往。子张说:"子夏是怎样说的?"回答说:"子夏说:'人品可以的就跟他交往,人品不可以的就加以拒绝。'"子张说:"不同于我所听到的:君子尊重贤人,也包容广大的普通人;赞美好人,也同情无能的人。我自己如果很好,对于别人有什么容不下的?我自己如果不好,人家将拒绝跟我交往,我又怎么能拒绝别人呢?"

【英译】

A disciple of Zi Xia's asked Zi Zhang about ways to associate with other people. Zi Zhang asked, "What has your teacher said about this?" The disciple answered, "Associate with those who have high moral standing, and reject those who do not." Zi Zhang said, "That is different from what I have learned, which is: A man of virtue respects the virtuous, but at the same time tolerates the ordinary; he compliments on the good, but at the same time sympathizes with the less capable. If I myself am good, what can't I tolerate about others? On the contrary, if I myself were not good, then other people would refuse to associate with me. So how could I reject other people anyway?"

Chapter Nineteen 子张第十九

子夏说："即使是一般小的知识与技艺，也一定有值得观摩的地方；只是要实现远大理想，唯恐陷进去受其拘泥，因此君子才不钻研它。"

Zi Xia said, "Even insignificant knowledge and small skills are worthy of being noted. A man of virtue has lofty ideals, so he does not study small skills lest he should be hindered in his great ambitions."

【释义】

子夏说："即使是一般小的知识与技艺，也一定有值得观摩的地方；只是要实现远大理想，唯恐陷进去受其拘泥，因此君子才不钻研它。"

【英译】

Zi Xia said, "Even insignificant knowledge and small skills are worthy of being noted. A man of virtue has lofty ideals, so he does not study small skills lest he should be hindered in his great ambitions."

19.4

zǐ xià yuē　　suī xiǎo dào　　bì yǒu kě guān zhě yān　　zhì yuǎn kǒng nì
子夏曰："虽小道，必有可观者焉；致远恐泥，
shì yǐ jūn zǐ bù wéi yě
是以君子不为也。"

子张第十九　Chapter Nineteen

【释义】

子夏说："每天能知道一些原来不知道的，每月都能不忘掉已经学会的东西，可以说是好学了。"

【英译】

Zi Xia said, "If a man learns new things every day and repeated reviewing what he has learned every month, then he can be said as fond of learning."

子夏说："每天能知道一些原来不知道的，每月都能不忘掉已经学会的东西，可以说是好学了。"

Zi Xia said, "If a man learns new things every day and repeated reviewing what he has learned every month, then he can be said as fond of learning."

19.5 子夏曰："日知其所亡，月无忘其所能，可谓好学也已矣。"

Chapter Nineteen 子张第十九

子夏说："广泛地学习而又不断坚定自己的意志，好问而又好思，仁也就在这里面了。"

Zi Xia said, "Learn extensively and strengthen your will constantly, ask questions earnestly and be diligent in thinking, then you are within the reach of virtue."

【释义】

子夏说："广泛地学习而又不断坚定自己的意志，好问而又好思，仁也就在这里面了。"

【英译】

Zi Xia said, "Learn extensively and strengthen your will constantly, ask questions earnestly and be diligent in thinking, then you are within the reach of virtue."

19.6
zǐ xià yuē　　bó xué ér dǔ zhì　　qiè wèn ér jìn sī　　rén zài qí
子夏曰："博学而笃志，切问而近思，仁在其
zhōng yǐ
中矣。"

子张第十九　Chapter Nineteen

【释义】

子夏说："各种工匠住在作坊里来完成自己的工作，君子通过学习来掌握道。"

【英译】

Zi Xia said, "Craftsmen complete their work by practicing in workshops, and men of virtue try to reach the Way by learning."

19.7
zǐ xià yuē　　bǎi gōng jū sì yǐ chéng qí shì　jūn zǐ xué yǐ zhì
子夏曰："百工居肆以成其事，君子学以致
qí dào
其道。"

Chapter Nineteen 子张第十九

子夏说："小人犯了错误，必定会加以掩饰。"

Zi Xia said, "For a petty-minded man, whenever he makes a mistake, he will try to cover it up."

【释义】

子夏说："小人犯了错误，必定会加以掩饰。"

【英译】

Zi Xia said, "For a petty-minded man, whenever he makes a mistake, he will try to cover it up."

19.8
zǐ xià yuē　　　xiǎo rén zhī guò yě　bì wén
子夏曰："小人之过也必文。"

子夏说:"君子有三变:远看他,庄重且令人敬畏;走近他,温和可亲;听他讲话,则很严肃。"

Zi Xia said, "A man of virtue leaves three different impressions on people in three different situations. From a distance, he appears serious and respectable; when close to him, he appears cordial and amiable; when he speaks, he sounds solemn."

19.9

zǐ xià yuē　　jūn zǐ yǒu sān biàn　　wàng zhī yǎn rán　　jí zhī yě wēn
子夏曰:"君子有三变:望之俨然,即之也温,
tīng qí yán yě lì
听其言也厉。"

【释义】

子夏说:"君子有三变:远看他,庄重且令人敬畏;走近他,温和可亲;听他讲话,则很严肃。"

【英译】

Zi Xia said, "A man of virtue leaves three different impressions on people in three different situations. From a distance, he appears serious and respectable; when close to him, he appears cordial and amiable; when he speaks, he sounds solemn."

Chapter Nineteen 子张第十九

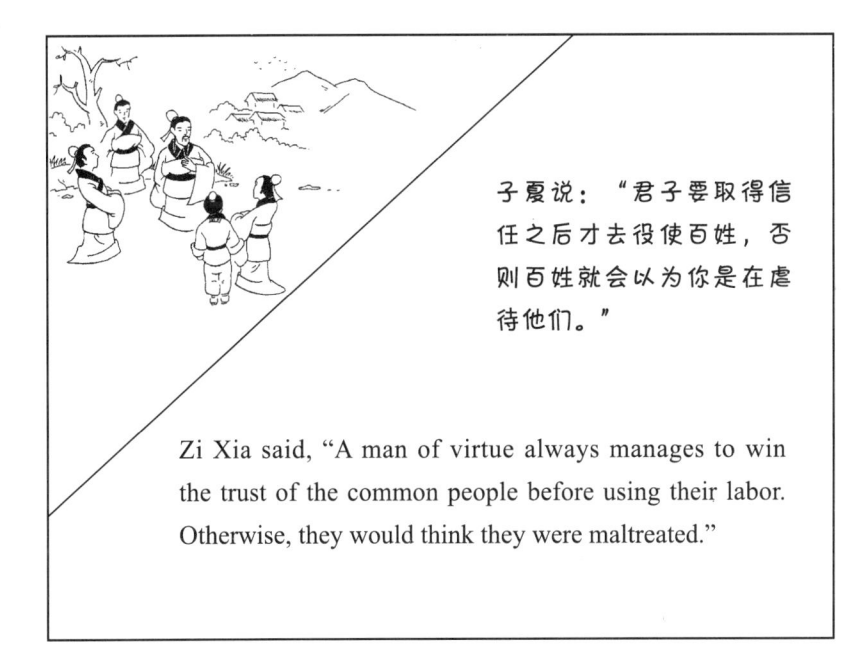

子夏说："君子要取得信任之后才去役使百姓，否则百姓就会以为你是在虐待他们。"

Zi Xia said, "A man of virtue always manages to win the trust of the common people before using their labor. Otherwise, they would think they were maltreated."

【释义】

子夏说："君子要取得信任之后才去役使百姓，否则百姓就会以为你是在虐待他们。君子要取得信任之后才去进谏君主，否则君主就会以为你是在诽谤他。"

【英译】

Zi Xia said, "A man of virtue always manages to win the trust of the common people before using their labor. Otherwise, they would think they were maltreated. A man of virtue always manages to win the trust of the monarch before remonstrating them. Otherwise, the monarch would take the remonstration as slander."

19.10 子夏曰："君子信，而后劳其民；未信，则以为厉己也。信而后谏，未信，则以为谤己也。"

子张第十九　Chapter Nineteen

【释义】

子夏说:"大节不越出界限,小节有所出入是可以的。"

【英译】

Zi Xia said, "As long as within the boundary of principles, it is acceptable to make flexible adjustments of details."

子夏说:"大节不越出界限,小节有所出入是可以的。"

Zi Xia said, "As long as within the boundary of principles, it is acceptable to make flexible adjustments of details."

19.11 zǐ xià yuē　　　dà dé bù yú xián　xiǎo dé chū rù kě yě
子夏曰:"大德不逾闲,小德出入可也。"

Chapter Nineteen　子张第十九

子夏说："对于小事末节和根本道理都能学通了的，恐怕只有圣人吧！"

Zi Xia said, "It is probably only the sages who can learn both small things and the fundamentals in a proper order from the beginning to the end."

19.12

子游曰："子夏之门人小子，当洒扫、应对、进退，则可矣，抑末也。本之则无，如之何？"

子夏闻之，曰："噫！言游过矣！君子之道，孰先传焉？孰后倦焉？譬诸草木，区以别矣。君子之道，焉可诬也？有始有卒者，其惟圣人乎！"

【释义】

子游说："子夏的弟子们，担当洒扫、应对、进退的工作那是可以的，但这些不过是礼仪的末节而已，论根本则没有，怎么办？"

子夏听到后，说："唉，子游说错了！君子的学问，哪些先传授，哪些后教诲呢？就和草木一样，都是分类区别的。君子的学问，怎么可以歪曲呢？至于能够有始有终，对于小事末节和根本道理都能学通了的，恐怕只有圣人吧！"

【英译】

Zi You said, "The disciples and followers of Zi Xia can deal with such small things as sprinkling water and cleaning the room, and welcoming and sending off guests. As for the fundamentals, they have not been taught. What should be done about this?"

Zi Xia heard this and said, "Alas! What Zi You said was wrong. In teaching the Way of men of virtue, there is an order as to what should be taught first and what should be taught next, just like the classification of grass and trees. How can one mislead the students when teaching the Way of men of virtue? It is probably only the sages who can learn both small things and the fundamentals in a proper order from the beginning to the end."

259

子张第十九　Chapter Nineteen

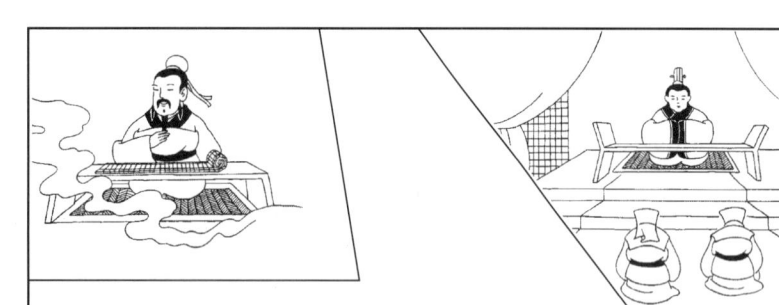

子夏说："做官而有余力的人，就可以去学习；学习而有余力的人，就可以去做官。"

Zi Xia said, "When an official has more time and energy left after fulfilling his duty, he should study; when a student has more time and energy left after fulfilling his studies, he should take office."

19.13
zǐ xià yuē　　shì ér yōu zé xué　　xué ér yōu zé shì
子夏曰："仕而优则学，学而优则仕。"

【释义】

子夏说："做官而有余力的人，就可以去学习；学习而有余力的人，就可以去做官。"

【英译】

Zi Xia said, "When an official has more time and energy left after fulfilling his duty, he should study; when a student has more time and energy left after fulfilling his studies, he should take office."

Chapter Nineteen 子张第十九

子游说："居丧能尽到悲哀之情也就够了。"

Zi You said, "When in mourning, one should stop at the point where he gives full expression of grief."

【释义】

子游说："居丧能尽到悲哀之情也就够了。"

【英译】

Zi You said, "When in mourning, one should stop at the point where he gives full expression of grief."

19.14 zǐ yóu yuē　　sāng zhì hū āi ér zhǐ
子游曰："丧致乎哀而止。"

子张第十九　Chapter Nineteen

【释义】

　　子游说："我的朋友子张已是难能可贵的了，但是还没有达到仁。"

【英译】

　　Zi You said, "What my friend Zi Zhang has achieved is rare, but he has not reached the standard of benevolence."

19.15

zǐ yóu yuē　wú yǒu zhāng yě　wéi nán néng yě　rán ér wèi rén
子游曰："吾友张也，为难能也，然而未仁。"

Chapter Nineteen　子张第十九

曾子说："子张仪表堂堂，但是难以跟他一起修养仁德。"

Zeng Zi said, "Zi Zhang is graceful and impressive in appearance, but it is hard to cultivate virtue along with him."

19.16

zēng zǐ yuē　　táng táng hū zhāng yě　　nán yǔ bìng wéi rén yǐ
曾子曰："堂堂乎张也，难与并为仁矣。"

【释义】

曾子说："子张仪表堂堂，但是难以跟他一起修养仁德。"

【英译】

Zeng Zi said, "Zi Zhang is graceful and impressive in appearance, but it is hard to cultivate virtue along with him."

子张第十九　Chapter Nineteen

曾子说："我听老师说过，人没有能自己竭尽其感情的，如果有，只有在父母去世的时候吧。"

Zeng Zi said, "I have heard this from my Master that a man very seldom shows his emotions to the full. The only occasion to do this may be at the mourning of his parents."

【释义】

曾子说："我听老师说过，人没有能自己竭尽其感情的，如果有，只有在父母去世的时候吧。"

【英译】

Zeng Zi said, "I have heard this from my Master that a man very seldom shows his emotions to the full. The only occasion to do this may be at the mourning of his parents."

19.17
zēng zǐ yuē　　　wú wén zhū fū zǐ　　rén wèi yǒu zì zhì zhě yě　　bì
曾子曰："吾闻诸夫子：人未有自致者也，必
yě qīn sāng hū
也亲丧乎！"

Chapter Nineteen 子张第十九

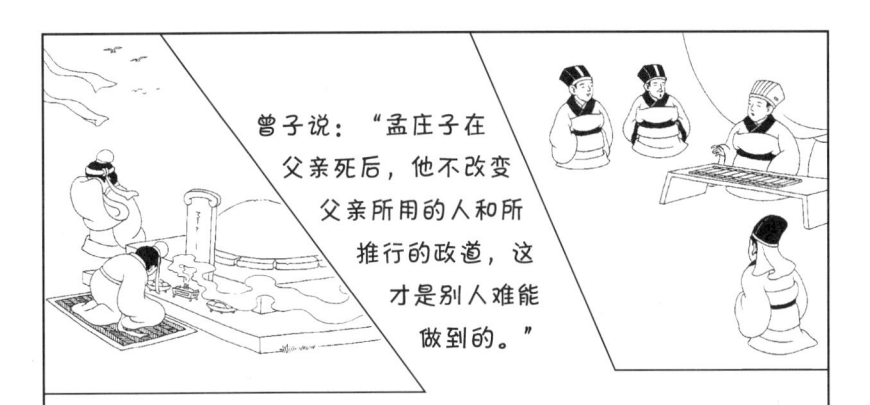

Zeng Zi said, "Meng Zhuangzi did not dismiss any of his father's officials, nor did he change the principles his father advocated. This is an example that is hard to follow."

19.18
zēng zǐ yuē wú wén zhū fū zǐ mèng zhuāng zǐ zhī xiào yě qí tā
曾子曰："吾闻诸夫子：孟 庄 子之孝也，其他
kě néng yě qí bù gǎi fù zhī chén yǔ fù zhī zhèng shì nán néng yě
可能也；其不改父之臣与父之政，是难能也。"

【释义】

曾子说:"我从老师那里听说过:孟庄子的孝,其他方面别人都可能做得到;在父亲死后,他不改变父亲所用的人和所推行的政道,这才是别人难能做到的。"

【英译】

Zeng Zi said, "I have heard this from my Master that about Meng Zhuangzi's filial piety, others may equal him in other aspects, but it is difficult to follow his example in not dismissing any of his father's officials and not changing the principles his father advocated."

子张第十九　Chapter Nineteen

曾子说："居上位的人做事失去道义，民心离散已经很久了。"

Zeng Zi said, "The rulers have led their governance astray, and the common people have long lost their trust in the authorities and have remained unguided."

19.19
mèng shì shǐ yáng fū wéi shì shī　wèn yú zēng zǐ　zēng zǐ yuē　shàng
孟 氏 使 阳 肤 为 士 师， 问 于 曾 子。 曾 子 曰："上
shī qí dào　mín sàn jiǔ yǐ　rú dé qí qíng　zé āi jīn ér wù
失 其 道， 民 散 久 矣。 如 得 其 情， 则 哀 矜 而 勿
xǐ
喜。"

【释义】

孟孙氏派阳肤做狱官，阳肤向曾子请教。曾子说："居上位的人做事失去道义，民心离散已经很久了。你如果了解了他们犯罪的真情，就要同情他们，而不要自喜。"

【英译】

The Meng family appointed Yang Fu as the chief criminal judge, and the latter asked for advice from Zeng Zi. Zeng Zi said, "The rulers have led their governance astray, and the common people have long lost their trust in the authorities and have remained unguided. So when you find out truth with the criminals, be sad and compassionate, and do not feel pleased with yourself."

Chapter Nineteen 子张第十九

子贡说:"商纣的暴虐,不像传说的这么厉害。所以君子厌恶身居低下的处境,一旦如此,天下的坏事都会推到他身上。"

Zi Gong said, "King Zhou of the Shang Dynasty was not as wicked as he was said to be. That is why a man of virtue hates to be held in low esteem, for if so, then all the evils in the world would be dumped on him."

【释义】

子贡说:"商纣的暴虐,不像传说的这么厉害。所以君子厌恶身居低下的处境,一旦如此,天下的坏事都会推到他身上。"

【英译】

Zi Gong said, "King Zhou of the Shang Dynasty was not as wicked as he was said to be. That is why a man of virtue hates to be held in low esteem, for if so, then all the evils in the world would be dumped on him."

19.20 子贡曰:"纣之不善,不如是之甚也。是以君子恶居下流,天下之恶皆归焉。"

子张第十九　Chapter Nineteen

子贡说："君子的过错就像日食、月食一样：犯错误时，人们都看得见；改正过错，人们都仰慕他。"

Zi Gong said, "The errors of a man of virtue are like eclipses of the sun or the moon. When he makes an error, everyone sees it; when he corrects the error, everyone looks up in admiration."

【释义】

　　子贡说："君子的过错就像日食、月食一样：犯错误时，人们都看得见；改正过错，人们都仰慕他。"

【英译】

　　Zi Gong said, "The errors of a man of virtue are like eclipses of the sun or the moon. When he makes an error, everyone sees it; when he corrects the error, everyone looks up in admiration."

19.21
zǐ gòng yuē　　jūn zǐ zhī guò yě　　rú rì yuè zhī shí yān　　guò
子贡曰："君子之过也，如日月之食焉：过
yě　rén jiē jiàn zhī　　gēng yě　　rén jiē yǎng zhī
也，人皆见之；更也，人皆仰之。"

Chapter Nineteen 子张第十九

子贡说："老师在哪里不能学呢？又为什么要有固定的老师呢？"

Zi Gong said, "From whom can't my teacher learn? And how could he possibly learn from only one single teacher?"

19.22
wèi gōng sūn cháo wèn yú zǐ gòng yuē　　zhòng ní yān xué　　zǐ gòng yuē
卫公孙朝问于子贡曰："仲尼焉学？"子贡曰：
wén wǔ zhī dào　　wèi zhuì yú dì　　zài rén　　xián zhě zhì qí dà zhě
"文武之道，未坠于地，在人。贤者识其大者，
bù xián zhě zhì qí xiǎo zhě　　mò bù yǒu wén wǔ zhī dào yān　　fū zǐ yān
不贤者识其小者。莫不有文武之道焉。夫子焉
bù xué　　ér yì hé cháng shī zhī yǒu
不学？而亦何常师之有？"

【释义】

卫国的公孙朝问子贡说："仲尼的学问是从哪里学来的？"子贡说："周文王、周武王的治道，没有失传，而是流传在民间。贤能的人能够了解其中的根本，不贤能的人只能了解其中的末节。到处都有文武之道存在。老师在哪里不能学呢？又为什么要有固定的老师？"

【英译】

Gongsun Chao from the State of Wei asked Zi Gong, "From whom did Confucius learn?" Zi Gong answered, "The Way of King Wen and King Wu of the Zhou Dynasty is not lost; it stays with the people. While the virtuous and talented focus on the fundamentals, the less virtuous and talented focus on trivialities. Either way, all of them benefit from the Way of King Wen and King Wu. From whom can't my teacher learn? And how could he possibly learn from only one single teacher?"

子张第十九 Chapter Nineteen

子贡说:"拿围墙来打比方,我的围墙跟肩头一样高,可以窥见房舍的美。老师家的围墙有好几丈高,如果找不到门走进去,就见不到宗庙的雄伟堂皇、房舍的多种多样。"

Zi Gong said, "Let's use the walls surrounding a mansion as an analogy. If my walls are as tall as a man's shoulder, above which one can see all the good things about the house, then my Master's walls are so tall that one can't see the magnificence of the mansion and its rich content unless one finds the gate and goes inside."

【释义】

叔孙武叔在朝廷中对朝中大夫说:"子贡比仲尼强。"

子服景伯把这话告诉了子贡。

子贡说:"拿围墙来打比方,我的围墙跟肩头一样高,可以窥见房舍的美。老师家的围墙有好几丈高,如果找不到门走进去,就见不到宗庙的雄伟堂皇、房舍的多种多样。能够找到门的人很少。武叔先生那样说,不也是自然的吗?"

【英译】

Shusun Wushu said to his fellow officials in court, "Zi Gong is better than Confucius."

Zifu Jingbo passed this along to Zi Gong.

Zi Gong said, "Let's use the walls surrounding a mansion as an analogy. If my walls are as tall as a man's shoulder, above which one can see all the good things about the house, then my Master's walls are so tall that one can't see the magnificence of the mansion and its rich content unless one finds the gate and goes inside. But since there are few people who can find the gate, isn't it only natural that Wushu made such a remark?"

19.23 叔孙武叔语大夫于朝曰:"子贡贤于仲尼。"
子服景伯以告子贡。
子贡曰:"譬之宫墙,赐之墙也及肩,窥见室家之好。夫子之墙数仞,不得其门而入,不见宗庙之美、百官之富。得其门者或寡矣。夫子之云,不亦宜乎?"

Chapter Nineteen 子张第十九

子贡说:"仲尼是不可以毁谤的。别人的贤能像是丘陵,还可以跨越;仲尼就像是日月,是不可能超越的。"

Zi Gong said, "Confucius is beyond slander. Other people's virtue is like a hill and can be surpassed, but the virtue of Confucius is like the sun or the moon; it can't be surpassed."

19.24

shū sūn wǔ shū huǐ zhòng ní   zǐ gòng yuē   wú yǐ wéi yě   zhòng ní
叔孙武叔毁仲尼。子贡曰:"无以为也!仲尼
bù kě huǐ yě   tā rén zhī xián zhě   qiū líng yě   yóu kě yú yě
不可毁也。他人之贤者,丘陵也,犹可逾也;
zhòng ní   rì yuè yě   wú dé ér yú yān   rén suī yù zì jué   qí
仲尼,日月也,无得而逾焉。人虽欲自绝,其
hé shāng yú   rì yuè hū   duō jiàn qí bù zhī liàng yě
何伤于日月乎?多见其不知量也。"

【释义】

叔孙武叔毁谤仲尼。子贡说:"不要这样做!仲尼是不可以毁谤的。别人的贤能像是丘陵,还可以跨越;仲尼就像是日月,是不可能超越的。人们即使想要自绝于日月,那对日月又有什么损害呢?只不过表示他不自量力罢了。"

【英译】

Shusun Wushu spoke ill of Confucius. Zi Gong said, "It is not wise to do such a thing. Confucius is beyond slander. Other people's virtue is like a hill and can be surpassed, but the virtue of Confucius is like the sun or the moon; it can't be surpassed. A man may want to isolate himself from the sun or the moon, but what harm can that do to the sun or the moon? It only shows his blindness to his own limitations."

子张第十九　Chapter Nineteen

子贡说："君子说一句话能够表现出睿智，同样一句话也能表现出愚蠢，讲话不可不谨慎啊。"

Zi Gong said, "A single utterance can reveal whether a man is wise or ignorant. Therefore, one should be cautious when making utterances."

19.25
chén zǐ qín wèi zǐ gòng yuē　　　　zǐ wéi gōng yě　　zhòng ní qǐ xián yú zǐ
陈子禽谓子贡曰："子为恭也，仲尼岂贤于子
hū
乎？"
zǐ gòng yuē　　　　jūn zǐ yì yán yǐ wéi zhì　　yì yán yǐ wéi bú zhì
子贡曰："君子一言以为知，一言以为不知，
yán bù kě bú shèn yě
言不可不慎也。"

【释义】

陈子禽对子贡说："您在仲尼面前表现得太谦恭了，仲尼难道真比您强吗？"

子贡说："君子说一句话能够表现出睿智，同样一句话也能表现出愚蠢，讲话不可不谨慎啊。"

【英译】

Chen Ziqin said to Zi Gong, "You are just being respectful, aren't you? Is Confucius really better than you?"

Zi Gong answered, "A single utterance can reveal whether a man is wise or ignorant. Therefore, one should be cautious when making utterances."

Chapter Nineteen 子张第十九

"夫子之不可及也，犹天之不可阶而升也。夫子之得邦家者，所谓立之斯立，道之斯行，绥之斯来，动之斯和。其生也荣，其死也哀。如之何其可及也？"

【释义】

"老师是不可匹及的，就像天一样高，是不可能凭借梯子登上去的。老师如果做了诸侯、大夫，就能做到。要树立仁，就能使百姓立于仁；要引导百姓，就能使百姓跟他走；要安抚百姓，就能使百姓来投奔；要动员百姓，就能得到众人响应。老师活着的时候就十分荣耀，死了之后又会使人悲哀。我怎么能赶得上他呢？"

【英译】

"My teacher can not be equaled, just like the sky can not be reached by climbing up a ladder. If my teacher had been in charge of the governance of a state or a noble family, then he would have achieved what is said in the saying: he advocates and things will last; he guides and people will follow; he brings comfort to people and people from the distance will come for submission; he initiates a move and people will work together in response. When my teacher lives, he honors the world. When he dies, all the people become sad. How could I be his equal?"

尧曰第二十
CHAPTER TWENTY

Chapter Twenty 尧曰第二十

宽厚就能得到众人的拥护，守信就能得到百姓的信任，勤敏就会取得成功，公平就会使众人愉悦。

Tolerance wins you the heart of the people, trustworthiness gains you others' trust, diligence leads to achievements, and fairness pleases the people.

20.1

yáo yuē　　　zī　ěr shùn　tiān zhī lì shù zài ěr gōng　yǔn zhí qí
尧曰："咨！尔舜！天之历数在尔躬，允执其
zhōng　sì hǎi kùn qióng　tiān lù yǒng zhōng
中。四海困穷，天禄永终。"
shùn yì yǐ mìng yǔ
舜亦以命禹。
yuē　　yú xiǎo zǐ lǚ　gǎn yòng xuán mǔ　gǎn zhāo gào yú huáng huáng
曰："予小子履，敢用玄牡，敢昭告于皇皇
hòu dì　yǒu zuì bù gǎn shè
后帝：有罪不敢赦。"

【释义】

尧说："啊！舜呀！天命已经落在你身上了，要真诚地坚持正确的道路。如果让天下人陷入贫穷，上天赐的禄位就会就此终结了。"

舜让位给禹的时候也用这话来告诫禹。

商汤说："我小子履，大胆虔诚地用黑色的公牛来祭祀，光明磊落地祭告伟大的天帝：我这个有罪之人不敢擅自赦免他们。"

【英译】

Yao (The ancient legendary emperor) said, "Shun! Heaven mandates that you should be my successor. Make sure to follow the way of centrality. If the world suffers hardship and poverty, then what Heaven bestows upon you will come to an end."

Shun gave the same advice to Yu when he passed the throne on to him.

King Tang of the Shang Dynasty said, "I, the humble Lü, venture to use a black bull for sacrifice, and venture to report to the great ruler of Heaven: I dare not pardon those who have committed crimes."

尧曰第二十　Chapter Twenty

"帝臣不蔽，简在帝心。朕躬有罪，无以万方；万方有罪，罪在朕躬。"

周有大赉，善人是富。"虽有周亲，不如仁人。百姓有过，在予一人。"

【释义】

"天帝的臣子如果有罪过也不敢隐瞒，天帝的心中是明白的。我自身如果有罪，不要因此连累天下万方；如果天下万方有罪，都由我一人承担。"

周朝赏赐天下，善人富有起来。武王也向天祷告说："即使有至亲，也不如有仁德的人。百姓如果有罪过，责任在我一人。"

【英译】

"And I dare not shield the crimes of the servants of the ruler of Heaven, either. The ruler of Heaven knows everything. If I am found guilty, please do not implicate other people in the world; but if other people in the world are found guilty, let me bear the responsibility."

During the Zhou Dynasty, a large number of people got grants and awards, and the good people became rich. King Wu said, "Although I have relatives who share the same surname with me, I'd prefer people of virtue. If the common people make mistakes, let the blame be on me alone."

Chapter Twenty 尧曰第二十

谨权量，审法度，修废官，四方之政行焉。兴灭国，继绝世，举逸民，天下之民归心焉。

所重：民、食、丧、祭。

宽则得众，信则民任焉，敏则有功，公则说。

【释义】

慎重制定重量和容量单位，审定长度单位，恢复废缺的职官，天下的政事也就行得通了。复兴灭亡的国家，接续断绝的世族，重用隐逸的贤人，天下的老百姓就会归服。

要重视的是：百姓、粮食、丧礼、祭祀。

宽厚就能得到众人的拥护，守信就能得到百姓的信任，勤敏就会取得成功，公平就会使众人愉悦。

【英译】

Strictly examine the weights and measures, perfect laws and regulations, and restore the official positions that have been cancelled, the governance in all parts of the country will be conducted smoothly. Rejuvenate the destroyed states, continue the extinct family lineage, and employ men of virtue who have lived in seclusion, then the common people in the world will submit to you with all sincerity.

Importance should be attached to the people, food, funerals and sacrificial ceremonies.

Tolerance wins you the heart of the people, trustworthiness gains you others' trust, diligence leads to achievements, and fairness pleases the people.

尧曰第二十　Chapter Twenty

孔子说："君子施恩惠于百姓却不浪费，役使人民却不被怨恨，有所欲求却不贪心，安详坦然却不骄傲，威严却不凶猛。"

The Master said, "A man of virtue is generous but not extravagant, capable of using the labor of the people without causing any resentment, desirous but not greedy, graceful without being arrogant, dignified but not fierce."

20.2

zǐ zhāng wèn yú kǒng zǐ yuē　　hé rú sī kě yǐ cóng zhèng yǐ
子张问于孔子曰："何如斯可以从政矣？"

zǐ yuē　　zūn wǔ měi　bǐng sì è　　sī kě yǐ cóng zhèng yǐ
子曰："尊五美，屏四恶，斯可以从政矣。"

zǐ zhāng yuē　　hé wèi wǔ měi
子张曰："何谓五美？"

zǐ yuē　　jūn zǐ huì ér bú fèi　láo ér bú yuàn　yù ér bù tān
子曰："君子惠而不费，劳而不怨，欲而不贪，

tài ér bù jiāo　wēi ér bù měng
泰而不骄，威而不猛。"

【释义】

子张询问孔子说："怎样做才能治理好政事呢？"

孔子说："尊崇五种美德，排除四种恶习，这样就可以治理好政事了。"

子张问道："五种美德是什么？"

孔子说："君子施恩惠于百姓却不浪费，役使人民却不被怨恨，有所欲求却不贪心，安详坦然却不骄傲，威严却不凶猛。"

【英译】

Zi Zhang asked, "What qualifications are required for conducting governance?" The Master answered, "Advocate the Five Merits and discard the Four Evils, then one can conduct governance."

Zi Zhang asked, "What are the Five Merits?"

The Master answered, "A man of virtue is generous but not extravagant, capable of using the labor of the people without causing any resentment, desirous but not greedy, graceful without being arrogant, dignified but not fierce."

Chapter Twenty 尧曰第二十

子张曰："何谓惠而不费？"

子曰："因民之所利而利之，斯不亦惠而不费乎？择可劳而劳之，又谁怨？欲仁而得仁，又焉贪？君子无众寡、无小大、无敢慢，斯不亦泰而不骄乎？君子正其衣冠，尊其瞻视，俨然人望而畏之，斯不亦威而不猛乎？"

【释义】

子张又问："什么叫施恩惠于百姓却不浪费？"

孔子说："百姓能够得利的事情而引导他们得利，这不就能做到施恩惠却不浪费吗？选择可以役使百姓的事情和时机来役使他们，这不就能做到不让百姓心存怨恨吗？想得到仁就得到了仁，还贪求什么呢？君子无论人多人少、事大事小，从不敢怠慢，这不就是庄重却不骄傲吗？君子衣冠端庄，仪表高贵，让人望而生畏，这不就是威严而不凶猛吗？"

【英译】

Zi Zhang asked further, "What is meant by being generous but not extravagant?"

The Master explained, "If one benefits the people by asking them to do what they can, isn't this being generous but not extravagant? If one chooses the right task and opportune time to use the labor of the people, then who will harbor resentment? If one is bent on the pursuit of virtue and achieves virtue, then what can he be greedy for? A man of virtue never slights anyone, be it a big crowd or a small group, and he never neglects anything, be it big or small. Isn't this being graceful without being arrogant? By being neatly dressed, a man of virtue appears dignified, impressive and awe-inspiring, isn't this being dignified but not fierce?"

尧曰第二十　Chapter Twenty

子张曰："何谓四恶？"

子曰："不教而杀谓之虐；不戒视成谓之暴；慢令致期谓之贼；犹之与人也，出纳之吝谓之有司。"

【释义】

子张问道："四种恶习是什么？"

孔子说："不加教育便行杀戮，叫做虐；不加以告诫，只看重成果，叫做暴；政令松懈，而期限紧迫，叫做贼；同是给人财物，出手十分吝啬，叫做小气。"

【英译】

Zi Zhang asked, "What are the Four Evils?"

The Master answered, "Cruelty—to kill people for their crimes without educating them first; brutality—to demand achievements without advance warning; banditry—to be lax in orders at the beginning but impose urgent deadlines later on; stinginess—to act in a miserly way when giving things out."

Chapter Twenty 尧曰第二十

孔子说："不懂得天命，就无法成为君子；不懂得礼制，就无法立足；不懂得分辨别人的言语，就无法了解别人。"

The Master said, "A man who does not know the Mandate of Heaven can never become a man of virtue; a man who does not know the etiquette will not be able to establish himself in society; a man who is incapable of judging other people's words can not understand the people."

【释义】

孔子说："不懂得天命，就无法成为君子；不懂得礼制，就无法立足；不懂得分辨别人的言语，就无法了解别人。"

【英译】

The Master said, "A man who does not know the Mandate of Heaven can never become a man of virtue; a man who does not know the etiquette will not be able to establish himself in society; a man who is incapable of judging other people's words can not understand the people."

20.3

kǒng zǐ yuē　　bù zhī mìng　wú yǐ wéi jūn zǐ yě　bù zhī lǐ
孔子曰："不知命，无以为君子也；不知礼，
wú yǐ lì yě　bù zhī yán　wú yǐ zhī rén yě
无以立也；不知言，无以知人也。"

281

图书在版编目（CIP）数据

漫画《论语》.下：汉英对照 / 于健主编.—北京：
北京语言大学出版社，2011.6
（中国国学经典学习丛书）
ISBN 978-7-5619-3046-5

Ⅰ.① 漫… Ⅱ.① 于… Ⅲ.① 论语–通俗读物–汉、英
Ⅳ.① B222.2-49

中国版本图书馆CIP数据核字（2011）第114833号

书　　名：	漫画《论语》（下）
责任印制：	汪学发

出版发行：北京语言大学出版社

社　　址：	北京市海淀区学院路15号	邮政编码：	100083
网　　址：	www.blcup.com		
电　　话：	国内发行 8610-82303650/3591/3651	海外发行	8610-82300309/0361/3080/3365
	编辑部 8610-82303647/3592	读者服务部	8610-82303653/3908
	网上订购电话 8610-82300090	客户服务信箱	service@blcup.net
印　　刷：	北京联兴盛业印刷股份有限公司		
经　　销：	全国新华书店		

版　　次：	2011年6月第1版　2011年6月第1次印刷
开　　本：	889毫米×1194毫米　1/24　印张：12
字　　数：	305千字
书　　号：	ISBN 978-7-5619-3046-5 / H·11086
定　　价：	35.00元

凡有印装质量问题，本社负责调换。电话：8610-82303590